MASTER THE™ DSST®

Human Resource Management Exam

About Peterson's®

Peterson's has been your trusted educational publisher for over 50 years. It's a milestone we're quite proud of, as we continue to offer the most accurate, dependable, high-quality educational content in the field, providing you with everything you need to succeed. No matter where you are on your academic or professional path, you can rely on Peterson's for its books, online information, expert test-prep tools, the most up-to-date education exploration data, and the highest quality career success resources—everything you need to achieve your education goals. For our complete line of products, visit **www.petersons.com.**

For more information, contact Peterson's, 4380 S. Syracuse St., Suite 200, Denver, CO 80237; 800-338-3282 Ext. 54229; or visit us online at **www.petersons.com**.

© 2020 Peterson's

ISBN: 978-0-7689-4456-3

Printed in the United States of America

10 9 8 7 6 5 4 3 2 1   22 21 20

Contents

Before You Begin

HOW THIS BOOK IS ORGANIZED

Peterson's *Master the*™ *DSST*® *Human Resource Management Exam* provides a diagnostic test, subject-matter review, and a post-test.

- **Diagnostic Test**—Twenty multiple-choice questions, followed by an answer key with detailed answer explanations
- **Assessment Grid**—A chart designed to help you identify areas that you need to focus on based on your test results
- **Subject-Matter Review**—General overview of the exam subject, followed by a review of the relevant topics and terminology covered on the exam
- **Post-test**—Sixty multiple-choice questions, followed by an answer key and detailed answer explanations

The purpose of the diagnostic test is to help you figure out what you know—or don't know. The twenty multiple-choice questions are similar to the ones found on the DSST exam, and they should provide you with a good idea of what to expect. Once you take the diagnostic test, check your answers to see how you did. Included with each correct answer is a brief explanation regarding why a specific answer is correct, and in many cases, why other options are incorrect. Use the assessment grid to identify the questions you miss so that you can spend more time reviewing that information later. As with any exam, knowing your weak spots greatly improves your chances of success.

Following the diagnostic test is a subject-matter review. The review summarizes the various topics covered on the DSST exam. Key terms are defined; important concepts are explained; and when appropriate, examples are provided. As you read the review, some of the information may seem familiar while other information may seem foreign. Again, take note of the unfamiliar because that will most likely cause you problems on the actual exam.

After studying the subject-matter review, you should be ready for the post-test. The post-test contains sixty multiple-choice items, and it will serve as a dry run for the real DSST exam. There are complete answer explanations at the end of the test.

OTHER DSST® PRODUCTS BY PETERSON'S

Books, flashcards, practice tests, and videos available online at **www.petersons.com/testprep/dsst**

- A History of the Vietnam War
- Art of the Western World
- Astronomy
- Business Mathematics
- Business Ethics and Society
- Civil War and Reconstruction
- Computing and Information Technology
- Criminal Justice
- Environmental Science
- Ethics in America
- Ethics in Technology
- Foundations of Education
- Fundamentals of College Algebra
- Fundamentals of Counseling
- Fundamentals of Cybersecurity
- General Anthropology
- Health and Human Development
- History of the Soviet Union
- Human Resource Management
- Introduction to Business
- Introduction to Geography
- Introduction to Geology
- Introduction to Law Enforcement
- Introduction to World Religions
- Lifespan Developmental Psychology
- Math for Liberal Arts
- Management Information Systems
- Money and Banking
- Organizational Behavior
- Personal Finance
- Principles of Advanced English Composition
- Principles of Finance
- Principles of Public Speaking
- Principles of Statistics
- Principles of Supervision
- Substance Abuse
- Technical Writing

Like what you see? Get unlimited access to Peterson's full catalog of DSST practice tests, instructional videos, flashcards and more for **75% off the first month**! Go to **www.petersons.com/testprep/dsst** and use coupon code **DSST2020** at checkout. Offer expires July 1, 2021.

Chapter 1

All About the DSST® Exam

WHAT IS DSST®?

Previously known as the DANTES Subject Standardized Tests, the DSST program provides the opportunity for individuals to earn college credit for what they have learned outside of the traditional classroom. Accepted or administered at more than 1,900 colleges and universities nationwide and approved by the American Council on Education (ACE), the DSST program enables individuals to use the knowledge they have acquired outside the classroom to accomplish their educational and professional goals.

WHY TAKE A DSST® EXAM?

DSST exams offer a way for you to save both time and money in your quest for a college education. Why enroll in a college course in a subject you already understand? For more than 30 years, the DSST program has offered the perfect solution for individuals who are knowledgeable in a specific subject and want to save both time and money. A passing score on a DSST exam provides physical evidence to universities of proficiency in a specific subject. More than 1,900 accredited and respected colleges and universities across the nation award undergraduate credit for passing scores on DSST exams. With the DSST program, individuals can shave months off the time it takes to earn a degree.

The DSST program offers numerous advantages for individuals in all stages of their educational development:

- Adult learners
- College students
- Military personnel

1

Adult learners desiring college degrees face unique circumstances—demanding work schedules, family responsibilities, and tight budgets. Yet adult learners also have years of valuable work experience that can frequently be applied toward a degree through the DSST program. For example, adult learners with on-the-job experience in business and management might be able to skip the Business 101 courses if they earn passing marks on DSST exams such as Introduction to Business and Principles of Supervision.

Adult learners can put their prior learning into action and move forward with more advanced course work. Adults who have never enrolled in a college course may feel a little uncertain about their abilities. If this describes your situation, then sign up for a DSST exam and see how you do. A passing score may be the boost you need to realize your dream of earning a degree. With family and work commitments, adult learners often feel they lack the time to attend college. The DSST program provides adult learners with the unique opportunity to work toward college degrees without the time constraints of semester-long course work. DSST exams take two hours or less to complete. In one weekend, you could earn credit for multiple college courses.

The DSST exams also benefit students who are already enrolled in a college or university. With college tuition costs on the rise, most students face financial challenges. The fee for each DSST exam starts at $80 (plus administration fees charged by some testing facilities)—significantly less than the $750 average cost of a 3-hour college class. Maximize tuition assistance by taking DSST exams for introductory or mandatory course work. Once you earn a passing score on a DSST exam, you are free to move on to higher-level course work in that subject matter, take desired electives, or focus on courses in a chosen major.

Not only do college students and adult learners profit from DSST exams, but military personnel reap the benefits as well. If you are a member of the armed services at home or abroad, you can initiate your post-military career by taking DSST exams in areas with which you have experience. Military personnel can gain credit anywhere in the world, thanks to the fact that almost all of the tests are available through the internet at designated testing locations. DSST testing facilities are located at more than 500 military installations, so service members on active duty can get a jump-start on a post-military career with the DSST program. As an additional incentive, DANTES (Defense Activity for Non-Traditional Education Support) provides funding for DSST test fees for eligible members of the military.

More than 30 subject-matter tests are available in the fields of Business, Humanities, Math, Physical Science, Social Sciences, and Technology.

Available DSST® Exams

Business	Social Sciences
Business Ethics and Society	A History of the Vietnam War
Business Mathematics	Art of the Western World
Computing and Information Technology	Criminal Justice
Human Resource Management	Foundations of Education
Introduction to Business	Fundamentals of Counseling
Management Information Systems	General Anthropology
Money and Banking	History of the Soviet Union
Organizational Behavior	Introduction to Geography
Personal Finance	Introduction to Law Enforcement
Principles of Finance	Lifespan Developmental Psychology
Principles of Supervision	Substance Abuse
	The Civil War and Reconstruction

Humanities	Physical Sciences
Ethics in America	Astronomy
Introduction to World Religions	Environmental Science
Principles of Advanced English	Health and Human Development
Composition	Introduction to Geology
Principles of Public Speaking	

Math	Technology
Fundamentals of College Algebra	Ethics in Technology
Math for Liberal Arts	Fundamentals of Cybersecurity
Principles of Statistics	Technical Writing

As you can see from the table, the DSST program covers a wide variety of subjects. However, it is important to ask two questions before registering for a DSST exam.

1. Which universities or colleges award credit for passing DSST exams?
2. Which DSST exams are the most relevant to my desired degree and my experience?

Knowing which universities offer DSST credit is important. In all likelihood, a college in your area awards credit for DSST exams, but find out before taking an exam by contacting the university directly. Then review the list of DSST exams to determine which ones are most relevant to the degree you are seeking and to your base of knowledge. Schedule an appointment with your college adviser to determine which exams best fit your degree program and which college courses the DSST exams can replace. Advisers should also be able to tell you the minimum score required on the DSST exam to receive university credit.

DSST® TEST CENTERS

You can find DSST testing locations in community colleges and universities across the country. Check the DSST website (**www.getcollegecredit. com**) for a location near you or contact your local college or university to find out if the school administers DSST exams. Keep in mind that some universities and colleges administer DSST exams only to enrolled students. DSST testing is available to men and women in the armed services at more than 500 military installations around the world.

HOW TO REGISTER FOR A DSST® EXAM

Once you have located a nearby DSST testing facility, you need to contact the testing center to find out the exam administration schedule. Many centers are set up to administer tests via the internet, while others use printed materials. Almost all DSST exams are available as online tests, but the method used depends on the testing center. The cost for each DSST exam starts at $80, and many testing locations charge a fee to cover their costs for administering the tests. Credit cards are the only accepted payment method for taking online DSST exams. Credit card, certified check, and money order are acceptable payment methods for paper-and-pencil tests.

Test takers are allotted two score reports—one mailed to them and another mailed to a designated college or university, if requested. Online tests generate unofficial scores at the end of the test session, while individuals taking paper tests must wait four to six weeks for score reports.

PREPARING FOR A DSST® EXAM

Even though you are knowledgeable in a certain subject matter, you should still prepare for the test to ensure you achieve the highest score possible. The first step in studying for a DSST exam is to find out what will be on the specific test you have chosen. Information regarding test content is located on the DSST fact sheets, which can be downloaded at no cost from **www. getcollegecredit.com**. Each fact sheet outlines the topics covered on a subject-matter test, as well as the approximate percentage assigned to each topic. For example, questions on the Human Resource Management exam are distributed in the following way: An Overview of the Human Resource Management Field—8%, Human Resource Planning—9%, Staffing/Talent Acquisition—11%, Training and Development—8%, Performance Management (Appraisals)—12%, Compensation and Benefits/Total Rewards—12%, Safety and Health—9%, Employment Law—16%, Labor Relations—10%, Current Issues and Trends—5%.

In addition to the breakdown of topics on a DSST exam, the fact sheet also lists recommended reference materials. If you do not own the recommended books, then check college bookstores. Avoid paying high prices for new textbooks by looking online for used textbooks. Don't panic if you are unable to locate a specific textbook listed on the fact sheet; the textbooks are merely recommendations. Instead, search for comparable books used in university courses on the specific subject. Current editions are ideal, and it is a good idea to use at least two references when studying for a DSST exam. Of course, the subject matter provided in this book will be a sufficient review for most test takers. However, if you need additional information, it is a good idea to have some of the reference materials at your disposal when preparing for a DSST exam.

Fact sheets include other useful information in addition to a list of reference materials and topics. Each fact sheet includes subject-specific sample questions like those you will encounter on the DSST exam. The sample questions provide an idea of the types of questions you can expect on the exam. Test questions are multiple-choice with one correct answer and three incorrect choices.

The fact sheet also includes information about the number of credit hours ACE has recommended be awarded by colleges for a passing DSST exam score. However, you should keep in mind that not all universities and colleges adhere to the ACE recommendation for DSST credit hours. Some institutions require DSST exam scores higher than the minimum score recommended by ACE. Once you have acquired appropriate reference materials and you have the outline provided on the fact sheet, you are ready to start studying, which is where this book can help.

TEST DAY

After reviewing the material and taking practice tests, you are finally ready to take your DSST exam. Follow these tips for a successful test day experience.

1. **Arrive on time.** Not only is it courteous to arrive on time to the DSST testing facility, but it also allows plenty of time for you to take care of check-in procedures and settle into your surroundings.
2. **Bring identification.** DSST test facilities require that candidates bring a valid government-issued identification card with a current photo and signature. Acceptable forms of identification include a current driver's license, passport, military identification card, or state-issued identification card. Individuals who fail to bring proper identification to the DSST testing facility will not be allowed to take an exam.
3. **Bring the right supplies.** If your exam requires the use of a calculator, you may bring a calculator that meets the specifications. For paper-based exams, you may also bring No. 2 pencils with an eraser and black ballpoint pens. Regardless of the exam methodology, you are NOT allowed to bring reference or study materials, scratch paper, or electronics such as cell phones, personal handheld devices, cameras, alarm wrist watches, or tape recorders to the testing center.
4. **Take the test.** During the exam, take the time to read each question-and-answer option carefully. Eliminate the choices you know are incorrect to narrow the number of potential answers. If a question completely stumps you, take an educated guess and move on—remember that DSSTs are timed; you will have 2 hours to take the exam.

With the proper preparation, DSST exams will save you both time and money. So join the thousands of people who have already reaped the benefits of DSST exams and move closer than ever to your college degree.

HUMAN RESOURCE MANAGEMENT EXAM FACTS

The DSST® Human Resource Management exam consists of 100 multiple-choice questions and is designed to evaluate whether candidates possess the knowledge and understanding that would be gained by taking a lower level college course in human resource management which includes the following content: overview of the human resource management field; human resource planning, staffing, training and development; performance appraisals; compensation issues; safety and security issues; employment law; and labor relations.

Area or Course Equivalent: Human Resource Management
Level: Lower-level baccalaureate
Amount of Credit: 3 Semester Hours
Minimum Score: 400
Source: https://www.getcollegecredit.com/wp-content/assets/factsheets/HumanResourceManagement.pdf

I. **An Overview of the Human Resource Management Field – 8%**

    a. Historical development

    b. Human resource functions

    c. The role and qualifications of the human resource manager

    d. Ethical aspects of human resource decision making

II. **Human Resource Planning – 9%**

    a. Strategic human resource issues

    b. Workforce diversity and inclusion

    c. Job analysis and job design

III. **Staffing / Talent Acquisition – 11%**

    a. Recruiting

    b. Selection

    c. Promotions and transfers

    d. Reduction-in-force

    e. Voluntary turnover, retirement, and succession planning

IV. **Training and Development – 8%**

    a. Onboarding

    b. Career planning

    c. Principles of learning

    d. Training programs and methods (e.g., Needs assessment, evaluation etc.)

    e. Development programs

V. **Performance Management (Appraisals) – 12%**

    a. Reasons for performance evaluation

    b. Techniques

    c. Challenges

VI. Compensation and Benefits / Total Rewards – 12%

    a. Job evaluation

    b. Wage and salary administration

    c. Compensation systems (e.g. Performance – related pay, executive compensation etc.)

    d. Benefits—mandatory and voluntary

VII. Safety and Health – 9%

    a. Occupational accidents and illness

    b. Quality of work life and wellness

    c. Workplace security

VIII. Employment Law – 16%

    a. Equal employment opportunity laws (e.g., Civil Rights Act Title VII, ADA, ADEA)

    b. Compensation and benefits related laws (e.g., ERISA, FMLA, FLSA)

    c. Health, safety and employee rights laws (e.g., OSHA, WARN)

IX. Labor Relations – 10%

    a. Role of labor unions

    b. Labor laws (e.g., NLRA, Taft-Hartley Act, Civil Service Reform Act)

    c. Collective bargaining

    d. Unionized versus non-unionized work settings

    e. Contract management

X. Current Issues and Trends – 5%

    a. Human resource information systems

    b. Changing patterns of work relationships (e.g., virtual office, contingent workers, autonomous work groups)

    c. Global HR environment

    d. Social Media

    e. Corporate social responsibility and sustainability

Chapter 2

Human Resource Management Diagnostic Test

DIAGNOSTIC TEST ANSWER SHEET

1. Ⓐ Ⓑ Ⓒ Ⓓ   8. Ⓐ Ⓑ Ⓒ Ⓓ   15. Ⓐ Ⓑ Ⓒ Ⓓ

2. Ⓐ Ⓑ Ⓒ Ⓓ   9. Ⓐ Ⓑ Ⓒ Ⓓ   16. Ⓐ Ⓑ Ⓒ Ⓓ

3. Ⓐ Ⓑ Ⓒ Ⓓ   10. Ⓐ Ⓑ Ⓒ Ⓓ   17. Ⓐ Ⓑ Ⓒ Ⓓ

4. Ⓐ Ⓑ Ⓒ Ⓓ   11. Ⓐ Ⓑ Ⓒ Ⓓ   18. Ⓐ Ⓑ Ⓒ Ⓓ

5. Ⓐ Ⓑ Ⓒ Ⓓ   12. Ⓐ Ⓑ Ⓒ Ⓓ   19. Ⓐ Ⓑ Ⓒ Ⓓ

6. Ⓐ Ⓑ Ⓒ Ⓓ   13. Ⓐ Ⓑ Ⓒ Ⓓ   20. Ⓐ Ⓑ Ⓒ Ⓓ

7. Ⓐ Ⓑ Ⓒ Ⓓ   14. Ⓐ Ⓑ Ⓒ Ⓓ

HUMAN RESOURCE MANAGEMENT DIAGNOSTIC TEST

24 minutes—20 questions

Directions: Carefully read each of the following 20 questions. Choose the best answer to each question and fill in the corresponding circle on the answer sheet. The Answer Key and Explanations can be found following this Diagnostic Test.

---

1. The field of industrial psychology is concerned with

    A. training management personnel.
    B. hiring and firing employees.
    C. employee testing and assignment.
    D. trade unions and collective bargaining.

2. Which of the following is NOT part of the strategic planning process for HRM?

    A. Identify employee skills that will enable the organization to attain its goals.
    B. Determine the organization's goals.
    C. Identify employees who exhibit desired skills.
    D. Create policies that will produce the desired employee skills.

3. Job evaluations are done by comparing

    A. salary incentives among employees in different departments.
    B. evaluations done by supervisory personnel.
    C. employee responses to exhaustive questionnaires.
    D. responsibilities and skills required for various jobs.

4. The human resource manager is expected to

    A. provide personalized and helpful service to customers.
    B. identify which workers deserve bonuses.
    C. plan the number of employees that an organization will need.
    D. give tours to visiting customers.

5. Which of the following is NOT included in employment law?

    A. Civil Rights Act Title VII
    B. Americans with Disabilities Act
    C. Family and Medical Leave Act
    D. Selective Service Act

6. Ergonomics covers such workplace issues as

    A. repetitive motion disorders.
    B. the prevention of food poisoning.
    C. traffic flow and overcrowding.
    D. the inhalation of hazardous gases.

7. In a structured job interview, the questioner will

    A. ask questions as he or she thinks of them.
    B. be joined by a panel of managers.
    C. expect certain acceptable responses.
    D. encourage the applicant to speak spontaneously.

8. Disciplinary action taken against a worker

    A. should not depend on the worker's seniority.
    B. may be more lenient with a first offender.
    C. usually begins with a verbal warning.
    D. is usually administered by the worker's union.

9. Which of the following is true about the Social Security Act of 1935?

    A. It is a voluntary benefit.
    B. It is a form of discretionary benefits.
    C. It is a means of workers' compensation.
    D. It is a mandatory benefit.

10. Which of the following is an example of a soft skills training topic?

    A. Time management strategies
    B. First aid techniques
    C. Current tax laws
    D. Manufacturing quality control

11. A recruiter is permitted to take into account an applicant's

    A. family responsibilities.
    B. previous work history.
    C. country of origin.
    D. posture and dress.

12. What right of workers does the Wagner Act of 1935 protect?

    A. Working in a closed shop
    B. Enacting right-to-work laws
    C. Choosing shop stewards
    D. Bargaining collectively

13. Which of the following is NOT a requirement of the Worker Adjustment and Retraining Notification Act (WARN)?

    A. Give 60 days advance notice of the closing of a plant.
    B. Notify the workforce of their right to organize in a union.
    C. Provide workers with retirement benefits.
    D. Close their business for all federal holidays.

14. Which of the following describes an apprenticeship program?

    A. New employees learn how to use simulated versions of the real equipment they will be working on.
    B. Employers provide informal training through coaching and on-the-job experience.
    C. New employees learn their jobs through on-the-job training and mentoring.
    D. New employees learn their jobs through a structured combination of classroom instruction and on-the-job training.

15. Any worker who leaves his or her home country to work in a foreign branch is a(n)

    A. third-country national.
    B. domestic worker.
    C. expatriate.
    D. agent.

16. Which of the following is the primary goal of OSHA?

A. Providing employee training
B. Preventing workplace accidents
C. Requiring employee health coverage
D. Monitoring corporate ethics

17. The passage of the Taft-Hartley Act marked a change from the way

A. legislation had favored unions.
B. states controlled the growth of unions.
C. legislation always favored management.
D. businesses bargained with unions.

18. A problem can arise with a performance evaluation if

A. the employee being assessed is about to retire.
B. the benefits administrator is not involved.
C. the supervisor shows bias in favor of some employees.
D. there have been multiple complaints about the supervisor.

19. Diversity in the workforce does NOT include being concerned with

A. perceived differences.
B. race, gender, or marital status.
C. varied lifestyles.
D. computer skills.

20. Which of the following describes a pay follower?

A. A firm that pays less than other companies in the same field
B. A firm that hires only the most experienced workers
C. A firm that rarely promotes anyone from the outside into management because of the pay differential
D. A firm that does not offer incentives to employees

ANSWER KEY AND EXPLANATIONS

1. C	5. D	9. D	13. B	17. A
2. C	6. A	10. A	14. D	18. C
3. D	7. C	11. B	15. C	19. D
4. C	8. C	12. D	16. B	20. A

1. **The correct answer is C.** The field of industrial psychology is concerned with employee testing and assignment. Choice A is incorrect because industrial psychology is not concerned with training. Choice B is incorrect because this field is not involved with hiring or firing workers. Choice D is incorrect because industrial psychology does not encompass trade unions and collective bargaining.

2. **The correct answer is C.** Identifying employees who already possess the skills and behaviors required to enable an organization to attain its goals is not part of HRM's strategic planning process. Choices A, B, and D are steps in the strategic planning process.

3. **The correct answer is D.** Job evaluations are done by comparing responsibilities and skills required for various jobs. Choice A is incorrect because incentives are not considered in job evaluations. Choice B is incorrect because there is likely to be only one supervisor involved. Choice C is incorrect because questionnaires are used for job analysis, not for performance appraisals.

4. **The correct answer is C.** The HR manager is expected to plan the number of employees that an organization will need. Choices A and D are incorrect because a human resource manager does not deal with customers. Choice D is also incorrect because that is likely to be done only in consultation with the direct supervisor. Choice B is incorrect because bonuses are determined by managers.

5. **The correct answer is D.** The Selective Service Act deals with military service and is not included in employment law. Employment law includes Title VII of the Civil Rights Act (choice A), the Americans with Disabilities Act (choice B), and the Family and Medical Leave Act (choice C).

6. **The correct answer is A.** Ergonomics involves fitting workplace conditions and job demands to the capabilities of workers. This covers accommodations for repetitive motion disorders. Food poisoning (choice B) and traffic flow and overcrowding (choice C) are not considered ergonomic issues. Choice D would be an OSHA (Occupational Safety and Health Administration) issue.

7. **The correct answer is C.** In a structured interview, the questioner will expect certain acceptable responses. Choice A is incorrect because asking random questions is not part of a structured interview. Choice B is incorrect because a panel of interviewers is not an aspect of a structured job interview. Choice D is incorrect because answering spontaneously would defeat the aim of a structured interview, which requires only certain acceptable answers.

8. **The correct answer is C.** Disciplinary action taken against a worker usually begins with a verbal warning. Choice A is incorrect because seniority should not influence whether disciplinary action is taken or not, although a long-time employee with a spotless record may be treated more leniently than one with a series of infractions. Choice B is incorrect because although leniency for a first offense may be true in some cases, it is not a given. Choice D is incorrect because although the union may have set rules on discipline, the union is not involved in administering worker discipline.

9. **The correct answer is D.** The SSA is a mandatory benefit. It is not a voluntary benefit (choice A), nor is it a discretionary benefit (choice B). Workers' compensation (choice C) is a separate issue.

10. **The correct answer is A.** Soft skills, such as time management, problem solving, and interpersonal communication, are important to job success, but are not related to a specific type of job. Choice B would likely be covered in a safety course, while choices C and D would be addressed in professional training sessions.

11. **The correct answer is B.** A recruiter is permitted to take into account an applicant's previous work history. Choices A and C are incorrect because taking into account family responsibilities and an applicant's country of origin would be a form of bias. Choice D is incorrect because considering posture and dress might influence interviewers and would also be a form of bias.

12. **The correct answer is D.** The Wagner Act, also known as the National Labor Relations Board, protects the rights of workers to organize and bargain collectively. Choice A is incorrect because the Wagner Act does not deal with closed shops, which require union membership to work in a company. Choice B is incorrect because workers don't enact laws; legislatures do. Right-to-work laws are state laws that make it illegal to refuse to hire someone because he or she doesn't belong to a union. Choice C is incorrect because choosing a shop steward is a union membership decision that doesn't involve company management.

13. **The correct answer is B.** The right to organize is protected under the National Labor Relations Board Act, commonly known as the Wagner Act. Choices A, C, and D are covered by WARN.

14. **The correct answer is D.** Apprenticeship programs are formal structured programs that combine classroom learning with on-the-job training. Choice A describes vestibule training, not an apprenticeship program. Choices B and C say essentially the same thing and are both incorrect.

15. **The correct answer is C.** An expatriate is a worker who leaves his or her home country to work in a foreign branch. A third party national (choice A) comes neither from the home country of the global business, nor the host country of its branch. A domestic worker (choice B) is a citizen of the host country. While an agent may seem like a logical answer, choice D is incorrect because it doesn't fit the description in the question.

16. **The correct answer is B.** The Occupational Safety and Health Administration (OSHA) oversees workplace health and safety. The agency sets safety standards and ensures compliance to reduce the frequency and severity of workplace accidents, so choices A, C, and D are incorrect.

17. **The correct answer is A.** The Taft-Hartley Act changed the way legislation favored unions. Choice B is incorrect because states did not—and do not—control the growth of unions. Choice C is incorrect because the Taft-Hartley Act was a reaction to legislation that favored unions, not management. Choice D is incorrect because the Act did not directly affect collective bargaining.

18. **The correct answer is C.** A problem can arise if a supervisor shows bias in favor of some employees. Choice A is incorrect because retirement would not be an issue in an evaluation. Choice B is incorrect because the benefits administrator should not be involved in performance evaluations. Choice D is incorrect because although there may have been multiple complaints about the supervisor, they would be regarded as a separate issue.

19. **The correct answer is D.** This question is looking for the answer that doesn't fit. Computer skills is not a diversity issue. Perceived differences (choice A); race, gender, and marital status (choice B); and varied lifestyles (choice C) are issues of concern in creating diversity in the workplace, so they are all incorrect.

20. **The correct answer is A.** Pay followers are companies that pay less than their competitors. Choice B is incorrect because hiring the most experienced workers would more likely be true of a pay leader. Choices C and D are incorrect because although they may seem like possible answers, neither describes a pay follower.

DIAGNOSTIC TEST ASSESSMENT GRID

Now that you've completed the diagnostic test and read through the answer explanations, you can use your results to target your studying. Find the question numbers from the diagnostic test that you answered incorrectly and highlight or circle them below. Then focus extra attention on the sections dealing with those topics.

Human Resource Management		
Content Area	**Topic**	**Question #**
An Overview of the Human Resource Management Field	• Historical development • HR functions • Role/qualifications of the HR manager • Ethical aspects of HR decision making	1, 4
Human Resource Planning	• Strategic HR issues • Workforce diversity/inclusion • Job analysis and job design	2, 19
Staffing / Talent Acquisition	• Recruiting • Selection • Promotions and transfers • Reduction-in-force • Voluntary turnover, retirement, succession planning	7, 11
Training and Development	• Onboarding • Career planning • Principles of learning • Training programs and method • Development programs	10, 14
Performance Management (Appraisals)	• Reasons for performance evaluation • Techniques • Challenges	8, 18
Compensation and Benefits / Total Rewards	• Job evaluation • Wage and salary administration • Compensation systems • Benefits—mandatory/ voluntary	3, 20

Safety and Health	• Occupational accidents and illness • Quality of work life and wellness • Workplace security	6, 16
Employment Law	• Equal employment opportunity laws • Compensation and benefits related laws • Benefits—mandatory/voluntary • Health, safety, and employee rights laws	5, 9, 13
Labor Relations	• Role of labor unions • Labor laws • Collective bargaining • Unionized vs. nonunionized work settings • Contract management	12, 17
Current Issues and Trends	• HR information systems • Changing patterns of work relationships • Global HR environment • Social media • Corporate social responsibility and sustainability	15

Chapter 3

Human Resource Management Subject Review

AN OVERVIEW OF THE HUMAN RESOURCE MANAGEMENT FIELD

Human Resource Management (HRM) is concerned with a company's employees, that is, its human resources. The primary goal of HRM is to suggest ways to manage the workplace so that all personnel contribute to the overall success of the company and are appropriately compensated for their contributions.

Historical Development

One of the earliest forms of personnel management was known as **industrial welfare**. During the Industrial Revolution of the nineteenth century, legislation expanded the responsibilities of those concerned with supervising personnel. For example, new laws regulated the work hours of children and women, and supervisors were required to see that those laws were observed.

Other developments further influenced personnel management. Frederick Taylor, a US mechanical engineer, is considered to be the founder of what became known as **scientific management**. Taylor promoted incentive systems that rewarded workers for meeting or exceeding objectives. He believed that pay should be linked to productivity, thus motivating workers to earn more by being more productive.

Others were also at work on ideas to improve management. During World War I, the new field of industrial psychology was beginning to be applied to the workplace. **Industrial psychology** is the branch of applied psychology concerned with the effective management of a labor force. For example, testing was introduced to evaluate military personnel so that they would be assigned to appropriate tasks. After the war, employee testing and assignment became a standard procedure in private industry.

In the early part of the twentieth century, many companies began to establish departments whose purpose it was to ensure workers' productivity by increasing job satisfaction, which, in turn, would increase productivity. These departments would eventually evolve into what became known as personnel departments. At first, these departments were concerned mainly with hiring suitable employees, but as their responsibilities became more complex, many personnel departments evolved into the HRM departments of today.

Human Resource Functions

Management functions have gradually expanded beyond staffing and training and development. A modern human resources department may have to deal with many issues, including the following:

- Trade unions and collective bargaining
- Laws guaranteeing civil rights and equal opportunity employment
- Outsourcing
- Globalization
- Information technology
- Pensions and benefits
- The use of part-time and temporary employees
- Mergers and takeovers
- Federal, state, and local laws
- Flextime and job sharing
- Health care costs

In many organizations, HRM is considered a strategic partner in developing the business.

The Role and Qualifications of the Human Resource Manager

In the past, **human resource (HR) managers** primarily handled administrative tasks—hiring workers, processing payroll, and filling out forms. However, the role of HR managers has expanded over time to involve both administrative and strategic tasks. Staffing, developing workplace policies, administering compensation and benefits, facilitating employee growth and retention, upholding laws related to the workplace, and addressing worker safety issues are just some of the many issues handled by HR managers.

Effective HR managers work alongside other departments and managers to meet the needs of employees and the organization. In many organizations, HR managers work in consultation with line managers—those persons with the direct managerial responsibility for employees. HR managers and line managers jointly evaluate employee performance, determine training and development needs, and make decisions about promotions and transfers. In organizations in which HRM is used strategically, HR managers work with senior management to develop strategic goals for the organization and forecast future employment needs.

Successful HR managers possess a wide range of skills to juggle tasks, technology, and people on a daily basis. One of the most important skills needed is organization because HR managers handle personnel files, employee benefits, government paperwork, and many other types of information. Strong time management skills and personal efficiency support an HR manager's organizational capabilities. Negotiation skills are also essential since the HR department typically works with job candidates and current employees to reach salary terms that are acceptable to both parties. Problem-solving capabilities also facilitate success in the HR field because HR managers often work on the front lines handling conflicts between employees.

Strong communication skills are critical for most jobs and especially in the HR profession which involves interacting with both upper-level managers and employees on a regular basis. In addition to speaking in front of groups, HR managers must communicate verbally, in writing, and through social media platforms. Effective communication skills enable HR managers to motivate employees and help them set personal goals that align with company objectives. The ability to communicate clearly with employees and recognize their achievements demonstrates the kind of leadership skills expected of HR managers.

Ethical Aspects of Human Resource Decision Making

Ethics is a system of moral principles intended to govern a person's or group's behavior. In business, adhering to such a set of principles includes, but is not limited to, following laws and regulations. A major difficulty that the manager faces is the realization that while something may be legal, it is not necessarily moral. Because the goal of the company is to make a profit, the manager must decide whether an action that might be profitable is also morally justified, based on the company's ethical guidelines.

HR managers face ethical decisions every day, and sometimes it may not be easy to make those decisions. In interviewing a prospective employee, for example, the HR manager might have to decide whether to explain a potentially difficult situation the new employee would face, such as taking the place of a highly popular manager who was terminated. HR managers negotiate salaries, manage employee conflicts, evaluate employee performance, and handle other situations involving confidential information, so a strong ethical foundation is essential.

HUMAN RESOURCE PLANNING

The role of the HR department has changed greatly from the days of overseeing hiring and firing. Today's HR department is a strategic partner with upper management in setting goals and executing the company's strategic plan.

Strategic Human Resource Issues

An HR manager is expected to identify the employee skills and behaviors required to meet the company's goals now and in the future. For example, a company may focus on providing customers with personalized and helpful service. To implement this strategy, therefore, the company will seek to hire employees they feel have empathy for others. Training and rewards will center on meeting that goal and should reach every level in the company.

Evaluation of the strategy should be ongoing so that management can make adjustments as needed over time. HRM works closely with company management to carry out and monitor how well employees are achieving the projected goals.

Familiarity with department managers and personnel enables HR managers to understand the strengths and weaknesses of the workforce and to anticipate future staffing needs. Tools such as **trend analysis**, **ratio analysis**, and **scatter plots** help HR managers to forecast staffing requirements, which enables them to support the strategic goals of the organization more effectively. These tools present the needed information in the following ways:

- *Trend analysis* involves collecting and evaluating data to identify patterns (or trends) over a period of time that might affect future staffing needs, such as changes in work processes and procedures, or supply and demand changes within markets and industries.

- *Ratio analysis* is useful in forecasting growth-driven personnel needs. It involves determining the future demand for human resources by calculating the ratio between a particular business variable and the number of employees a company needs.

- *Scatter plots* are used to predict the relationship or demand between an organization's activities or departments and its staff levels. If a relationship between these two variables exists, the company's employee requirement can be estimated.

Depending on the goals of the organization, HR managers will need to evaluate the current staff, determine how many people to hire, when to hire them, and what skills the new workers should possess.

Strategic HR also involves developing compensation plans and reward systems that will attract and retain the best talent. Researching wage trends and monitoring the labor market provides the information needed to do this accurately. Developing training programs that equip employees for their jobs and support business goals are also important components of strategic HR plans. Strategic HRM optimizes an organization's human resources to ensure organizational success.

Workforce Diversity and Inclusion

The concept of **diversity** in the workforce has evolved over the years. Originally, its meaning was fairly narrow and mainly related to race and gender. Today diversity, which refers to the differences between people, also encompasses age, religion, disabilities, country of origin, marital status, socioeconomic status, family responsibilities, and sexual orientation. In terms of HRM, **diversity management** involves recognizing and proactively managing the unique needs of today's workforce and establishing an inclusive work environment often through policies and strategies. Being inclusive requires employers to be open-minded and supportive so that all employees feel welcome and valued. A cohesive workforce is one in which employees work well together. Prospective employees are drawn to a company with that kind of reputation, and customers benefit from the harmonious environment. As an added bonus, studies indicate that corporate bottom lines benefit from workforce diversity as well.

Job Analysis and Job Design

Job analysis and **job design** are part of the process of determining specific tasks to be performed, what methods are used in performing those tasks, and how the job relates to other work in the organization. Through this system, the HRM can identify the skills, duties, and knowledge necessary for performing certain jobs.

This process applies as new jobs are created or old ones are redesigned because of changing requirements or procedures. Job analysis and job design can provide information needed for staffing, training and development, compensation, and safety and health, all of which are crucial to the development of job descriptions. HRM might gather this information by means of observation, questionnaires, interviews, employee logs of their duties, or a combination of methods.

STAFFING AND TALENT ACQUISITION

Staffing includes a variety of aspects, such as recruitment and selection in order to ensure that an organization has the right employees in the right jobs to execute the company's strategic plan and achieve its goals.

Recruiting

Recruiting is a process. The first step is deciding, as part of planning and forecasting, what positions to fill. Next, recruiters have to build up a pool of candidates drawn from both internal and external sources. For internal recruiting, HRM consults personnel records to identify employees with the right skills set, and then interviews them for the position. The law requires jobs to also be posted, and workers may respond to job postings when they find a job description that seems to match their skills and experience.

Today's HR managers use a variety of methods to recruit externally. Job search websites like Indeed.com, Monster.com, and CareerBuilder.com are effective tools for posting available positions and identifying possible candidates. Social media also serves as a modern recruiting tool. LinkedIn, for example, the business-focused social networking site, enables HR managers to find and be introduced to potential job candidates. Some firms also use social media platforms like Facebook and Twitter to post jobs and engage with candidates. Other online recruiting options include the company website and professional association websites. More traditional methods such as job fairs, help-wanted ads, and college recruiting and internships allow recruiters to screen candidates for education, attitude, motivation, and communication skills.

Some firms also turn to outside sources for their recruitment needs. Executive search firms focus on filling upper-management and CEO positions and charge hefty fees for the task. If a business needs to fill a position temporarily, such as when a permanent employee takes medical leave, a staffing firm may be contacted.

Selection

How long the actual selection of staff takes can be affected by various factors, including company rules and legal considerations. Company rules on hiring and promotion may depend on the level of the position. For example, someone being considered for an executive position will probably be subject to more scrutiny than an applicant for a clerical position.

Legal considerations involve making sure that hiring is not discriminatory in any way and meets all the requirements of legislation governing hiring. HR managers must avoid potential problems related to intentional (**disparate treatment**) or unintentional (**disparate** or **adverse impact**) discrimination. **Adverse impact**, which refers to hiring practices that seem neutral but actually discriminate against a protected group, is estimated with the **four-fifths, (or 80%) rule** set by the EEOC's Uniform Guidelines on Employee Selection Procedures. For example, assume that a company has 100 total job applicants consisting of 80 males and 20 females, and the company selects 60 males and five females. Adverse impact is demonstrated because 75% of males were selected in comparison to 25% of women, and 25/75 equals 33%, which is less than the 80% requirement.

Even when the parties involved in the selection process are confident in their final choice, the candidate may be required to undergo a physical exam before being officially hired. Following up on references and checking the accuracy of resumes may also extend the vetting process.

Interviewing—structured or unstructured—makes up a significant part of the selection process. In an **unstructured interview**, interviewers ask questions as they think of them. For a **structured interview**, though, the types of questions are predetermined. Even responses that are considered acceptable are delineated in advance.

Some interview questions are intended to explore the applicant's job skills. For example: What courses did you take in college that involved using your organizational skills? Other questions might be more situational, such as asking how the person would react to certain circumstances. Or a question might call on an applicant to describe particular situations in his or her work experience and explain how the candidate handled them.

Applicants may have to submit to several interviews, gradually moving up the levels of management. Negotiation of compensation with the final candidates is also part of the interview process.

Some companies conduct panel interviews, with the candidate being interviewed simultaneously by a group of managers or peers who will be working with the candidate or a combination of both.

Promotions and Transfers

When promotions or transfers are considered for company personnel, HRM considers past experience and measurable competence. Still, there is no guarantee that even a high-performing employee will do as well in another position, which suggests that his or her future performance should be monitored in the first few months.

Transfers, which are usually lateral moves, generally mean being responsible for familiar tasks and decisions. Though such moves do not usually mean a higher paycheck, it may be desirable for the employee for other reasons. These might include better working hours, less commuting, or simply the need for a change of environment.

Reduction-In-Force

A **reduction-in-force**, or **RIF**, may be the result of such external factors as an economic downturn or a merger or buyout by another company. A RIF that follows a merger or buyout occurs because when the two companies combine, there is a duplication of some staff positions. An internal cause of downsizing might be a company's own plans for reorganizing its work groups or its business.

A RIF is generally permanent. A **layoff**, on the other hand, is the discharge, often temporary, of workers. Those employees may be rehired once economic conditions improve. To minimize layoffs during a downturn, a company may try reducing everyone's hours and scheduling periodic plant closings or unpaid vacations.

The HR department may be called on to conduct termination interviews in which department personnel break the news to terminated workers and explain their severance packages. A company may also provide outside help in the form of the services of an outplacement firm, which counsels the affected employees by providing instruction on how to strengthen their job-search skills and rewrite their resumes. Outplacement firms may also provide office space and some secretarial help for a period of time for affected employees.

The HR department also needs to deal with the "survivors," the employees who have retained their positions in a RIF situation. A RIF is likely to affect, at least temporarily, the morale of those left behind, challenging their sense of security. The more sensitively the HR department handles the situation, the better the adjustment the remaining staff will make.

Voluntary Turnover, Retirement, and Succession Planning

Because of the cost and time involved in recruiting and training new workers, companies remain alert to the rate of **employee turnover**. So, for example, when personnel from the HR department conduct exit interviews with workers who are resigning voluntarily, they will analyze the workers' responses to certain questions. The aim is to gain insight about why these people are leaving, including their perception of how the company has treated them. Information gathered this way may help the firm in the future to retain high-quality employees.

Retirement is another type of voluntary turnover, at least more so than it has been in the past. Though mandatory retirement age requirements still exist in some companies, there has been a trend in recent years toward **phased retirement**, which results in retirement being a process rather than an abrupt end to workers' jobs. Phased retirement allows workers to move gradually from full-time work to full retirement. They might begin by reducing the number of hours they work, gradually decreasing those hours over time. This may benefit the company, too, in that it allows management to reduce labor costs without the upheaval of a RIF. The benefit to older workers is that they can keep their benefits while working shorter hours.

Another way a firm may reduce its labor costs without laying off workers is by offering **early retirement** packages. These offer senior employees benefits that they would not receive if they retired later. However, workers do have the option of turning down such offers. There can also be a disadvantage to the company in making such offers. If it makes the offer to a whole class of workers (for example, senior employees), it risks losing some of its most experienced and able personnel.

With the growing number of retirements among the baby boomer generation, many firms are focusing their attention on succession planning. **Succession planning** prepares for the fact that turnover occurs by developing employees within the organization who can fill senior positions in the future. An effective succession plan identifies key positions and the potential personnel who could be groomed to fill those positions. By training, motivating, and developing such employees for senior positions, an organization ensures a smooth transition when current top executives retire or resign.

TRAINING AND DEVELOPMENT

A large segment of an HR manager's responsibilities involves the training and development of an organization's employees, from top management to hourly workers.

Onboarding

First impressions in business are important because it is within the first six months of employment that many new hires decide whether to stay or leave. Many firms develop employee onboarding programs to improve the retention rates of new hires. **Onboarding** refers to the process of integrating new employees into a firm and its culture and providing them with the necessary tools and information to be successful, productive, and engaged. In the past, many organizations focused only on new employee orientation, which is a component of onboarding that takes place during the first few days on the job and primarily involves completing paperwork and covering company history, policies, and procedures. However, onboarding is an ongoing process that can last for months with the objective of making new employees want to work at the firm.

The HR department is likely to be involved in onboarding, but other personnel may take part: (1) line managers wishing to establish a productive relationship with a new employee, and (2) peers who can anticipate a new employee's interests and concerns. Some employers may institute a buddy system, with a peer becoming a mentor to the new worker. Other employers may use a team approach, thus providing the newest member with ready access to different knowledge skills.

Career Planning

How an employee's career develops is important to both that worker and the company itself. **Career planning** is the ongoing process by which both the individual and the company are involved in that worker's development.

Self-assessment is a vital part of an employee's career planning. It involves recognizing one's interests, skills, and goals. Knowing one's strengths and weaknesses can help a person make the correct career choices and avoid mistakes that lead to job dissatisfaction. For example, if someone accepts a position that is not sufficiently challenging, it can lead to a bored employee making careless mistakes. On the other hand, the challenged worker who can apply his or her skills to a task and feel successful will not only find job satisfaction, but will also contribute to the company's success.

Some companies assist employees in planning their career paths by providing informative materials, personal guidance, and workshops. They might also compensate employees for approved outside courses, including those using e-learning and computer applications.

Principles of Learning

It probably is not logical to expect a single list of the principles of learning to apply to all learning situations. However, the following list recognizes the special requirements of the workplace:

- *Employee Motivation:* This can take many forms. The possibility of promotion, for example, can motivate employees to learn because employees will feel that their ability, training, and experience are likely to be recognized and rewarded.
- *Recognition of Individual Differences:* It is important that workers be rewarded for their particular capabilities by being assigned to learning tasks that recognize and challenge those abilities.
- *Transfer of Learning* (from one position to another): Workers can carry over certain skills from one assignment to another. A management that recognizes and acts on this fact prevents workers from being locked into one career path, especially if it is not a satisfying one.
- *Meaningful Materials:* Print, computer applications, DVDs, online programs, workshops—these are all available for educating workers. To be effective, materials should be up-to-date and directly related to the skills that learners need to master for their jobs. A review by supervisory personnel helps to ensure that the materials are current and appropriate to the company's and the workers' goals.

Management should also recognize that learning can take place both formally and informally. **Formal learning** may be company-sponsored or the result of individual initiative. It may take place in a classroom, workshop, or online. **Informal learning** is on-the-job learning, resulting from working and exchanging ideas with colleagues. It is an inexpensive form of learning, and companies are wise to encourage it.

An **apprenticeship** is another method for learning job-related knowledge and skills. It requires a combination of formal instruction and on-the-job training by a knowledgeable staff member with good communication skills.

Training Programs and Methods

Training includes all those activities designed to provide learners with the knowledge and skills they need to do well in their present jobs. Companies with a reputation for encouraging learning are at an advantage in several ways. For one, training and development programs help in recruiting new workers concerned about how they will advance during their tenure at a company. It is likely, too, that a reputation for learning will attract more highly qualified applicants.

To be successful in today's workplace, employees need to be able to manage time and communicate well, solve difficult problems, work both independently and as a member of a team, and to accept and thrive in a constantly changing environment. In general, these and other skills, referred to as **soft skills**, are not taught in college and university classes., but because they are vital to an organization's success, HRM will often include soft skills training in its training and development programs, in addition to any measurable **hard skills** (e.g., math, programming, and technical) training it may deem necessary.

Any training must be done in context—the context being a **needs assessment**, or an analysis of the company's actual needs. HRM must ask itself the following types of questions:

- Which workers need to be trained?
- What do they need to learn?
- What do they need to do differently from what they are doing now?
- Will this training help advance the goals of the organization?

Training methods vary from company to company and include instructor-led sessions, online training, virtual classrooms, and case studies. Perhaps the most common one is a class led by an instructor. This method is especially effective with a small group and an instructor who encourages lively discussion. **Online**, or **e-learning**, delivered by computer or mobile device has become more and more popular. It not only allows more flexibility in terms of time and distance, but it is also cost-effective once the program is developed. A typical training session ends with a survey to elicit feedback on the effectiveness of the training.

One method often used for management training is the **case study**. A group leader presents a simulated situation in which a manager is required to analyze the case and then suggest solutions to the problem. The leader must be able to keep the discussion positive and productive. Role-playing and business games similarly involve participants' decision-making skills.

Development Programs

Development programs are also concerned with learning, but they center on the skills and knowledge that go beyond the trainee's present job. Development involves individual career planning within the context of organizational development. **Human resource development** is a major responsibility of the HR department.

Management development seminars and conferences may emphasize such skills as assertiveness training for women, cost accounting, and developing emotional intelligence. While these might not be the types of courses one would find in a college curriculum, they may enhance a management candidate's qualifications for a supervisory position.

As a further stimulus to improving management skills, a company might employ executive coaches from an outside firm. The coach identifies the candidate's strengths and weaknesses, and then helps that executive capitalize on his or her strengths. **Coaching**, while expensive, has proven to be effective, as shown by assessments from both subordinates and supervisors.

PERFORMANCE MANAGEMENT

Pay, promotion, and retention are based on performance appraisals. These evaluations are the way a firm's employees become aware of their standing in the company. **Performance appraisals** are formal evaluations as opposed to the ongoing assessment of employees' performance that managers should be conducting.

Reasons for Performance Evaluation

Long before the performance appraisals are actually carried out, the process should begin with the supervisor setting the **performance standards**, or criteria, which employees are expected to meet. These standards should be based on the following: (1) appropriate traits, such as attitude and appearance; (2) appropriate behaviors, such as diligence and organizational skill; (3) competencies, such as business knowledge and interpersonal skills; (4) achievement of goals; and (5) potential for improvement. Once the appraisals have been conducted, the supervisor works with employees to develop a plan to eliminate any deficiencies. If a worker performs well, he or she will benefit from immediate feedback.

Similarly, if worker performance is less than ideal, the sooner the worker receives feedback, the sooner he or she can, in conjunction with the supervisor, take the necessary steps to improve performance.

Techniques

A variety of performance evaluation techniques are used by firms. Some companies use a **grading method**, which uses a packed form, either paper or online, that lists the areas on which the employee is to be graded. The types of rankings may vary. For example, the supervisor may have to choose a number from 1 to 7 that he or she believes best represents the employee's progress, with the highest number representing the highest achievement. Another approach, the **management by objectives (MBO) method**, involves a supervisor judging an employee on the basis of whether previously defined objectives have been met. The **360-degree approach** requires gathering performance feedback from co-workers, customers, direct reports, and managers. The **Behaviorally Anchored Rating Scales (BARS)** method compares employee performance against specific job-related behaviors. Assessment centers use multiple evaluation tools to evaluate employees, while the **critical incident method** requires managers to document specific examples of exceptional performance and examples of less-than-stellar performance.

Challenges

Performance appraisals are supposed to be based on fair-minded criteria, but they are subjective, and biases and stereotyping can creep in. A manager may be too lenient with one worker and too strict with another. If an employee's view of his or her performance is more positive than the supervisor's evaluation, it can result in a perception of unfair treatment. Also, the evaluation process can be manipulated if the manager wishes to favor one employee or disparage another.

On the other hand, some of the unpleasantness of a poor performance appraisal can be avoided if managers handle problems, such as repeated lateness, as they occur rather than waiting several months to act on issues that need correction. Day-to-day communication and corrective measures can prevent crises from occurring during formal evaluations.

Disciplinary Procedures

Prior to termination, there are procedures for dealing with infractions, and it may fall to the HR manager to administer discipline to workers who do not come up to company standards or have failed to follow company rules. The disciplinary action usually occurs only after all other strategies to improve the workers' performance have failed.

Disciplinary actions may take different approaches. It is a given, though, that the action cannot be personal; that is, it should not show either bias or favoritism. Also, the disciplinary action should be taken immediately. It should not be delayed, for example, until the employee's next review, which might be weeks or months away.

Though company rules should be administered consistently, it is realistic to assume that the HR manager might act differently depending on circumstances. For example, if dealing with a first infraction by a new employee, the HR manager might be more lenient in his or her approach. Likewise, if a long-time employee's record has been exemplary until this infraction, the manager might correct the employee's behavior without administering a penalty. Flexibility then becomes a matter of judgment.

Ideally, the manager would apply the minimum penalty to any first offender. The manager would also have to balance the need to avoid damaging employee morale with making sure that all employees understand the need to follow company rules.

The sequence of disciplinary steps begins with a verbal warning, followed, if necessary, by a written warning. Beyond that, the HR manager would have to consider whether the situation warrants suspension or termination. Another alternative is demotion, usually with a reduction in pay. In a union situation, this must be handled according to the firm's agreement with the union.

Whatever the resolution, the HR manager should handle any disciplinary action with consideration for the employee's likely emotional reaction as well as that of his or her colleagues. In all cases, the manager's interaction with the employee should be private and never carried out in front of others.

Termination

Termination requires sensitivity and honesty, with the manager explaining what actions warranted the termination. Where there is a union agreement, the manager must follow the rules governing termination with cause. Before it comes to this end, though, it is important that the manager keep in mind that it may be more expensive to hire a replacement than to retain an experienced worker who might only need a period of readjustment.

COMPENSATION, BENEFITS, AND TOTAL REWARDS

Compensation is the pay and rewards, such as money bonuses or stock awards, which employees get in exchange for their work. Compensation may be direct or indirect. **Direct compensation** includes salary, wages, commissions, and bonuses, whereas **indirect compensation** includes benefits such as paid vacations, holidays, and medical insurance. In order to attract, motivate, and retain effective employees, many firms offer total rewards packages that consist of compensation, health and dental insurance, performance bonuses, stock options, company-sponsored training, wellness programs, flexible schedules, employee discount programs, and many other perks and benefits.

Job Evaluation

Job evaluation is the formal and systematic comparison of a firm's positions. The comparison is designed to determine the value of one job in relation to others. Basically, it attempts to compare the effort, responsibility, and skills required to perform each job. Compensation for each position is then based on this evaluation.

The process begins with the creation of a **job analysis** for each position. This information is then used to prepare a **job description**. HRM might then assign rankers to rank the jobs. The rankers must be consistent in the factors they use to make their rankings. Once they have sorted the job descriptions, using the standard of ranking the most difficult job as the highest, the next step may be to assign each rank to a particular pay grade. A **pay grade** is made up of all jobs that fall within a certain range.

Rankers work independently of one another, but then meet to adjust and average the ratings. When the wages are plotted on a graph, they should reveal a wage curve that can show the relative value of and the average wage for each job.

Of course, most companies do not pay just one rate for all jobs in a particular pay grade. Instead, there may be several levels, or steps, within each pay grade. Finally, an employer must account for individual circumstances (such as years of service) before establishing a pay rate for each worker.

Wage and Salary Administration

Clearly, the task of administering wages is complex. The compensation manager in the Human Resources department is responsible for recommending financial compensation by establishing pay rates for various grades. In determining direct financial compensation, the manager must take into account the following factors:

- The company's policies on salaries
- The ability of the company to pay
- Employee job performance
- Employee skills and competencies
- Employee experience
- Employee potential
- Labor union contracts
- Legislation
- Economy
- Cost of living
- Job evaluations

In addition to evaluating these criteria in-house, an administrator has the option of accessing various internet sites that report on what other firms are paying for comparable jobs. These sites also report on benefits. Besides private, commercial firms, businesses can consult the U.S. Department of Labor's Bureau of Labor Statistics online database of compensation for various industries.

Compensation Systems

The systems that govern decisions on compensation vary from company to company. These compensation policies provide managers with general guidelines for making decisions about compensation. Based on these decisions, a company might fall into one of three categories:

1. *Pay Leaders:* Those firms that pay higher compensation than their competitors. Higher-paying companies then logically expect to attract the most highly qualified workers.
2. *Market Rate:* Also called the going rate. This is the rate perceived to be the average for similar jobs in the industry.
3. *Pay Followers:* Companies that pay less than their competitors. The decision to pay less may be based on the firm's financial condition. It could also reflect the fact that the firm does not believe it requires highly qualified workers.

While these compensation policies indicate a desire to ensure consistency, other factors can alter a policy. For example, there may be pressure to retain high performers through the inducement of a higher salary and/or generous benefits. Other factors that affect such decisions include the following:

- The labor market of potential employees
- Labor unions and their contracts with employers
- The current economy
- Legislation regulating some salaries

The distinction between exempt and nonexempt workers is an example of legislation that affects compensation. By law, companies are expected to adhere to a government policy of classifying workers as either exempt or nonexempt. **Exempt workers** are those salaried employees categorized as executive, administrative, professional, or outside salespeople. **Nonexempt employees**, on the other hand, receive an hourly wage and are covered by laws regulating minimum wage, overtime, and other rights and protections.

Many companies offer incentive plans that, under certain circumstances, give employees additional compensation beyond their salaries or hourly pay. Salespeople, for example, may receive a fixed salary plus commissions for sales that meet or surpass a set quota. Such sales commissions are an example of performance related pay.

Other programs recognize worker achievements by awards that may or may not be monetary in nature. These can include **employee stock ownership plans** (**ESOP**), gift certificates, and merchandise, as well as profit-sharing plans and cash rewards. Some publicly traded firms offer **executive compensation** in the form of bonuses and stock options to CEOs, CFOs, managing directors, and other upper-level managers for their efforts on behalf of the organization.

Benefits: Mandatory and Voluntary

The compensation manager is also expected to administer indirect financial compensation, or benefits. Some benefits are mandatory while individual firms initiate others. Examples of **mandatory**, or legally required, benefits include the following:

- *Social Security:* The original Social Security Act of 1935 was created to provide benefits for retired workers. Amendments to the Act have since added other kinds of protection for workers.
   - *Disability insurance* provides for workers who are completely disabled.
   - *Survivors' benefits* help a worker's survivors—the widow or widower and unmarried children—if the employee dies. *Medicare* offers hospital and medical insurance for workers over 65.

Although the retirement age to be eligible for Social Security benefits has gradually risen over the years, eligibility for Medicare benefits remains age 65 for most people. Employees and employers contribute to the Social Security fund.

- *Unemployment Compensation:* If workers lose their jobs through no fault of their own, they become eligible for unemployment compensation, a joint federal-state program. This insurance program provides temporary benefits payments for a certain number of weeks, typically up to 26 weeks or until the worker finds another job, whichever comes first. It is funded by a payroll tax paid by employers. In times of severe economic downturn, Congress may extend the compensation period as it did during the recession that began in 2007. While the federal government provides guidelines for the program, it is administered by the states. This means that the benefits, including the time period, can vary from one state to another.
- *Workers' Compensation:* If a worker incurs expenses due to a job-related accident or illness, he or she can be reimbursed through this program. Workers' comp, as it is commonly called, also provides some income replacement. Employers purchase the insurance independently through private insurance companies, but the program is subject to federal regulation and is administered by the states.

Discretionary benefits are a form of indirect financial compensation, and individual employers can decide which to offer. The same factors that determine the level of direct compensation—salaries, wages, commissions, and bonuses—influence the types and amount of discretionary benefits employees receive. Some of the most common discretionary benefits include the following:

- Paid vacations
- Sick pay
- Medical benefits
- Life insurance
- Retirement plans
- Stock option plans
- Childcare
- Scholarships for dependents

Retirement plans may be one of two types: defined benefits and defined contribution. A **defined benefits plan** gives retirees a specific amount of income upon retirement. It may be a lump sum or a monthly pension amount and is funded by employers. Under a **defined contribution plan**, employees don't receive a specific amount of money to fund their retirement. They contribute a portion of their salary toward retirement and employers may or may not also contribute. A 401(k) plan is an example of a defined contribution plan.

Another type of indirect compensation is the voluntary benefit. **Voluntary benefits** are those offered to employees by a company, but for which employees have to pay because the company feels it cannot afford to do so. However, the company usually pays the administrative costs, and employees benefit because they pay a group rate. These include the following:

- Term life insurance
- Vision insurance
- Long-term care insurance
- Dental insurance
- College savings plans

SAFETY AND HEALTH

Workers' safety and health are important to companies because lost time on the job cuts into productivity, raises health-care costs, and could lead to lawsuits, depending on the nature and cause of the injuries. **Safety** refers to protecting employees from physical injury on the job, and health is the physical and mental well-being of employees.

Occupational Accidents and Illness

The **Occupational Safety and Health Act of 1970** was passed specifically to ensure worker safety and health in the United States. It established the

Occupational Safety and Health Administration (OSHA) that works with employers to create good working environments. The agency's rules and regulations have helped eliminate many workplace-related fatalities, injuries, and illnesses and reduced the cost to companies of such injuries and illnesses.

If an employee feels endangered by conditions in the workplace, he or she may complain to OSHA, thus possibly initiating an OSHA inspection. The Act protects any employee who requests an inspection, refuses unsafe work, or complains about a dangerous workplace. If the OSHA inspector finds unsafe conditions, this can result in financial penalties for the company. Follow-up inspections check to make sure that the recommendations for improvement have been followed. If conditions have not improved, this results in further penalties.

While it is probably impossible to eliminate every cause of injury or illness on the job, companies can focus on the following areas to reduce hazards and the organization's liability:

- *Unsafe Worker Behavior:* Safety promotion campaigns can improve worker attitudes. It is a fact that workers suffer more injuries when they are new to a job, so placing an emphasis on safety during the first few months of employment can have a significant effect.
- *Unsafe Working Conditions:* A company may find that it must alter working conditions to meet OSHA standards. Though worker safety is the company's responsibility, employees should be encouraged to suggest their own solutions to unsafe conditions. Management must inform all workers of any hazards and take steps to correct them.
- *Job Hazard Analysis (JHA):* JHA requires the assessment of work activities and the workplace to establish whether adequate precautions have been taken to prevent injuries. It involves the systematic identification of potential hazards in the workplace as a step to controlling the possible risks involved. OSHA provides online forms and checklists that employers can download and use to evaluate workplace conditions. Some hazards are obvious, like slippery floors in an area that has a great amount of foot traffic. Others are less so, requiring the kind of expertise a safety engineer can offer. Categories that are analyzed for hazards on such forms are fire prevention, work environment, working/walking surfaces, ergonomics, emergency information (postings), emergency exits, electrical systems, and material storage. The following are examples of OSHA questions relating to fire prevention. Respondents are asked to choose from three possible answers: Yes, No, and N/A (not applicable).
  - Are employees trained on the use of portable fire extinguishers?
  - Is heat-producing equipment used in a well-ventilated area?
  - Are fire alarm pull stations clearly marked and unobstructed?

- *Ergonomics:* Studying people's efficiency in their working environment and then designing the workplace so that employees can function without pain is called ergonomics (from the Greek word *ergon*, "work"). It requires fitting the machine or movements to the worker rather than asking the worker to make the adjustment to such stressful motions as twisting one's whole body. In this way, employers have been able to reduce repetitive motion disorders like carpal tunnel syndrome, bursitis, and tendonitis.
- *Accident Investigation:* It is important that firms investigate any accident; determine the cause; and take steps to prevent other, similar accidents. At the same time, collecting accurate data about accidents over a set period can be valuable, especially if this shows either an increase or a decrease in the frequency and severity of accidents.

Quality of Work Life and Wellness

Quality of work life can be defined as the extent to which employees can enhance their personal lives through their work environment and experiences. Healthy employees equate to less absenteeism, lower health-care costs, and increased productivity, so many organizations offer employee wellness programs that include vaccination clinics, nutrition education, exercise programs, health screenings, and substance abuse programs.

Additional policies and opportunities enhance the quality of work life:

- *Flextime:* Schedule flexibility
- *Compressed Work Week:* Allowing employees to work the same number of hours, but in fewer days
- *Telecommuting:* Working from home
- *Job Sharing:* Two part-time workers splitting one job
- *Part-Time Work:* Giving employees time to take care of personal needs
- A family-friendly workplace with childcare
- A generous benefits program

Workplace Security

A feeling of safety in the workplace has come to mean more than just job security. Unfortunately, there have been many cases of workplace violence. Some of the incidents have been carried out by angry workers against fellow employees. The perpetrators are often people who believe that they have not been treated well by management or who have been victims of bullying by the coworkers they are targeting.

Sometimes, violence is carried out by an outsider. Often, the outsider is not targeting the company, but aims to harm someone with whom he has had a personal relationship, such as an estranged wife or girlfriend. Women are the usual victims in these types of attacks. Even dissatisfied customers have been known to react violently to circumstances and attack employees of a company they have a grudge against. Robbery is also a problem for some companies, especially retail establishments.

HRM does have some options for reducing workplace violence, which include the following:

- Keep a minimal amount of cash on hand in retail businesses
- Install a silent alarm system to alert security
- Install surveillance cameras
- Train workers in conflict resolution
- Screen employees for a history of violent behavior, including sexual harassment
- Question unexplained gaps in an applicant's employment
- Check for criminal records involving violence
- Prohibit firearms or other weapons in the facility

Training supervisors to recognize employees who display a tendency to react aggressively to situations, threaten others, or demonstrate antisocial behavior may also prevent a worker from acting violently.

EMPLOYMENT LAW

Most employees are hired and hold their jobs at their employer's discretion, which is known as employment-at-will, meaning that neither party acknowledges a time limit on the employer–employee relationship. Therefore, either party can terminate the relationship, with due notice. There are, however, some limits on terminating an employee, for example, where legislation or union rules govern such actions. A wrongful termination suit brought by a terminated employee would have to be based on promises or guarantees made by the company, but not adhered to. Then it is up to the claimant to prove that such assurances were made. As the following table shows, there are several laws that govern employee management. There are four categories of employment laws: equal employment; compensation and benefits; health, safety, and employee rights; and union laws. An HR manager needs to be familiar with all of them in order to see that they are administered properly.

Employment Laws

Equal Employment Laws

Civil Rights Act Title VII	Makes it unlawful for an employer to discriminate against any individual because of race, color, religion, sex, or national origin
Americans with Disabilities Act (ADA)	Prohibits discrimination against workers with disabilities employed by certain federal contractors and subcontractors
Age Discrimination in Employment Act (ADEA)	Prohibits discrimination against workers within certain age ranges, the ranges changing as the law is amended

Compensation and Benefits

Employment Retirement Income Security Act (ERISA)	Sets minimum standards for pension programs in private industry to protect employees' contributions
Family and Medical Leave Act (FMLA)	Provides certain employees with up to 12 weeks of unpaid leave under certain circumstances related to family needs
Fair Labor Standards Act (FLSA)	Sets provisions for minimum wage, maximum hours, conditions for overtime pay, equal pay, recordkeeping, and child labor; distinguishes between exempt and non-exempt employees

Health, Safety, and Employee Rights

Occupational Safety and Health Act of 1970	Requires employers to provide a safe and healthy working environment
Worker Adjustment and Retraining Notification Act (WARN)	Requires 60 days advance notice of a plant closing or mass layoff

Union Laws

National Labor Relations Act (NLRA)	Supports the right of labor to organize and engage in collective bargaining
Taft-Hartley Act	Prohibits unfair union labor practices, enumerates the rights of employees and employers, allows the U.S. president to bar national emergency strikes
Civil Service Reform Act	Regulates most labor management relations in the federal service

LABOR RELATIONS

A union is an organization of workers who find strength in coming together to deal with their employer. Generally, unions organize because of dissatisfaction with management policies. They strive to improve wages, hours, working conditions, and benefits for their members.

Role of Labor Unions

Although unions, or at least associations of workers, have been in the United States since the eighteenth century, it was not until the 1930s that unions in the United States began to grow in members and in significance. Until then, lawmakers and court decisions had favored management. But then, during the Great Depression, millions of workers were unemployed, and those who had jobs, especially factory jobs, worked long hours for little pay in unsafe and unhealthful working conditions.

The 1930s saw the passage of several laws that strengthened the rights of workers to organize and of unions to negotiate for their members. Probably the most important of these laws was the National Labor Relations Act of 1935 (also known as the **Wagner Act**, after Robert F. Wagner, then a US Senator from New York, who sponsored the bill). The NLRA protected the rights of workers to organize and to bargain collectively.

After the passage of the Wagner Act, union membership showed a large increase. However, public attitudes shifted after several costly strikes following World War II. Although then-president Harry Truman vetoed the law, Congress overrode his veto to pass the Labor Management Relations Act, also known as the **Taft-Hartley Act**. The intention of the law was to allow for a more even-handed approach toward labor and management. It placed restrictions on both sides, but probably the most significant one was Section 14b, which allows states to pass **right-to-work laws** that restrict closed shops. In a **closed shop**, membership in a union is a condition for being hired and for continued employment.

Collective Bargaining

Since the Wagner Act was passed, both management and labor have been required, by law, to engage in **collective bargaining**. That is, they must sit down together to negotiate wages, hours, and terms and conditions of employment in good faith. While neither side is forced to accept any demands offered by the people on the other side of the table, it is expected that both sides will negotiate honorably, that is, with sincerity of intention;

in other words, "in good faith." Representing the union is the shop steward, a person elected by workers to represent them in these and other dealings with management.

Once the two sides have reached an agreement, the union membership must ratify the agreement. Once management and the union have approved of the deal, it becomes part of the contract between them for the period called for in the contract, usually about three years. A contract generally covers such issues as wages and overtime and such special situations as hazard pay, layoff or severance pay, holidays, vacations, and family care provisions. Grievance procedures, work breaks, strikes, and lockouts, as well as management rights are also covered. Items that may not be negotiated are discriminatory treatment of employees, separation of races in the workplace, and a closed shop. The latter requires that a worker join a union in order to be hired. All three are illegal.

Unionized Versus Nonunionized Work Settings

Management in nonunionized work situations probably look at their circumstances as easier than those in a company with a strong union. In a sense, that is the difference between an environment that allows collective bargaining and one that does not have that option. In the first case, bargaining is done by the shop steward on one side and management on the other. Because the shop steward is representing the interests of a whole class of people, the bargaining can be tough. On the other hand, where there is no union, the bargaining must be done on a person-by-person basis.

Contract Management

Most **collective bargaining agreements**, or **CBAs**, include grievance procedures to clarify the process for handling contract violations. While contracts and procedures vary, HR departments are typically involved in addressing grievances because of their knowledge about the specific contract and relevant laws. The first step in the grievance process usually involves a discussion between the manager, employee, HR representative, and union representative and results in a written decision from management. In some cases, grievances are escalated to the national union, and arbitrators are brought in to facilitate a mutual agreement.

CURRENT ISSUES AND TRENDS

HR departments must stay current with today's ever-changing work environments. In addition to those areas addressed previously, other trends in HRM that bear watching are the use of human resource information systems, changing patterns of work relationships, HR management in a global environment, ethical use of social media, and promoting corporate social responsibility and sustainability.

Human Resource Information Systems

Increasingly sophisticated technology is allowing companies to implement highly useful **human resource information systems (HRIS)**. An HRIS allows HR to collect and store, in one place, the vast amount of data it needs to research and track information about such things as recruitment and hiring, compliance with legislation and regulations, and the administration of the benefits program. It can identify the costs associated with various activities and present graphs to show inventory levels and disclose profit levels over a set period of time. It allows the production department to fill orders and accounting to bill the right customers in a timely manner. Employees may also have access to information about programs that they can enroll in, insurance coverage, benefits, and retirement plans.

Changing Patterns of Work Relationships

Changes in the workplace are a reflection of the varied lifestyles of the workforce. At one time, employers hired new workers, assigned them a workstation, and expected them to present themselves there at the usual starting time. Of course, such situations still occur, but many organizations are recognizing that younger workers desire a work–life balance and job flexibility. Technology has allowed for greater flexibility in work arrangements but also raises issues related to virtual offices, contingent workers, unconventional work arrangements, outsourcing, employee leasing, and training methods like e-learning and m-learning.

For example, with the **virtual office**, workers may not even have to appear in person, only electronically. A virtual office may be an actual place, but most importantly, it is equipped with telecommunication links that enable workers to connect. However, the office doesn't have to be a fixed place anymore. The computer itself can become the office, and its operator can function just about anywhere.

Contingent workers also have a nontraditional connection with a firm. The "contingency" is that they are subject to chance, that is, to the needs of the employer at a particular time. They may work as part-timers, temporary employees, or independent contractors. Their temporary availability allows the company flexibility and lower expenses than an on-site employee. There are none of the extra costs, such as vacation time or company contributions to medical insurance. The drawback for the employees, though, is that they are readily disposable. Still, companies that utilize contingent workers are going beyond the kind of workers needed only for unskilled jobs. The contingent workers can also be engineers, technicians, and specialists in various fields, including the law.

There are also other unconventional work arrangements. One is the **autonomous work group**. Under this arrangement, workers are part of a team that decides for itself how the work should be distributed among members of the team.

Outsourcing and employee leasing are other recent options in the business world. **Outsourcing** involves hiring workers outside the company to do work that was previously done in-house. **Employee leasing** is perhaps one of the more far-reaching alternatives to standard hiring practice. A company releases its employees, who are then hired by a professional employer organization (PEO). The PEO pays the workers and the expenses normally associated with permanent employees: workers compensation, payroll taxes, and employee benefits

Employees and employers also appreciate flexible training options, which can be cost effective for the organization and convenient for the employees. For example, training in the format of **electronic learning (e-learning)** allows employees to access online training and development programs. **Mobile learning**, known as **m-learning**, enables employees to access training programs via mobile devices like smartphones and laptops.

Global HR Environment

While conducting business in a global environment has become commonplace, it remains complex and challenging. An international HRM office becomes very important to an organization because it is vital that a company's staff be trained to handle the unique challenges of working globally. Among the factors that HRM on the global level must deal with are cultural, legal, and economic differences, as well as political risks.

Companies doing business in the global market may transfer personnel from their domestic offices to work in their satellite firms abroad. These workers are often called **expatriates**. In addition, US companies often hire nationals from their host countries or even third-country nationals. For this mixed group of people to work well together, there must be a common language, such as English. For the US workers, having a second language is a plus. In some cases, though, a translator may be necessary. Workers who remain in this country but interact with global offices may need training to work effectively in an international environment. Employees selected for overseas assignments receive orientation and training before departure and online training, development, and support while abroad. Coordination among offices in multiple countries frequently depends on email, instant messaging, and virtual meetings; differences in time zones are a consideration as well.

Of primary importance is the fact that management cannot assume that US ways of doing business are universal. Having different cultural and business backgrounds will affect the interactions between the US corporation and personnel from the host country, further reflecting the importance of training in cultural sensitivity. Managers and expatriates also need to be aware that not only are there likely to be cultural differences, but also political, legal, and economic ones. Consideration must also be given to helping the families of expatriates adjust to their new environment such as by finding jobs for spouses and schools for children.

Social Media

Another important trend that is crucial for HR managers to consider is the use of social media. Although many managers report anecdotally reviewing job applicants' social media sources prior to hiring, all aspects of the employee hiring process must be documented and validated. In other words, if a manager is reviewing a potential applicant's Facebook account, there must be documented evidence that the evaluation of the Facebook account is reliable (consistently measured) and valid (job-related). This is an important ethical issue that HR managers must consider to avoid potential problems related to intentional (disparate treatment) or unintentional (disparate impact) discrimination.

Corporate Social Responsibility and Sustainability

An increasing number of organizations are focusing on **corporate social responsibility (CSR)** and **sustainability**, and HR can play a key role in the implementation of such efforts, which need employee participation to be successful. Encouraging employees to participate in company-sponsored volunteer activities, creating recognition programs to celebrate employee efforts, encouraging green practices, and incorporating CSR into recruitment programs are just a few ways that HR managers can support CSR and sustainability.

SUMMING IT UP

- The field of **human resource management (HRM)** traces its roots back to the Industrial Revolution and a form of personnel management known as industrial welfare. Forerunners of contemporary HRM include the work of Frederick Taylor, industrial psychology, and personnel departments.
- Three primary human resource functions are **human resource planning, staffing and talent acquisition**, and **training and development**. Other responsibilities include **performance appraisals, compensation, safety and health issues, employee rights** and **discipline**, and **forecasting staffing**.
- HRM works with line managers, employees, and senior management.
- Effective HR managers are **organized**, possess strong **negotiation skills**, and **communicate clearly**.
- HR departments may be used as a strategic partner with upper management to set goals and execute an organization's strategic plan. HRM assists by predicting future staffing needs through the use of **trend analysis, ratio analysis**, or **scatter plots**, as well as **forecasting** the training needs that will be required.
- **Diversity management** involves recognizing and proactively managing the unique needs of today's workforce and establishing an inclusive work environment often through HR policies and strategies.
- **Job analysis** and **job design** are part of the process of determining specific tasks to be performed, the methods to be used in performing those tasks, and how the job relates to other work in the organization.
- **Staffing** involves **recruiting, selection, promotions** and **transfers, reduction-in-force, layoffs**, and **voluntary turnover**. Candidates may come from internal or external sources. Selection of staff can be influenced by company rules and legal considerations. Voluntary turnovers may occur because of resignations and retirements.
- **Onboarding** is the process of integrating new employees into an organization and its culture and giving them the tools and information to be successful, productive, and engaged.
- **Principles of learning** that need to be recognized in the workplace include the need to motivate employees, recognition of individual differences in learning, the ability of employees to transfer learning, and the need to provide meaningful materials.
- **Training methods** today can take a variety of forms, including instructor-led sessions, online training, virtual classrooms, and case studies. One-on-one coaching may also be appropriate.
- **Development programs** center on the skills and knowledge that go beyond the trainee's present job to deal with career planning.

- Pay, promotion, and retention are based on **performance appraisals**, which are formal evaluations of an employee as opposed to the ongoing assessment of performance that managers should be conducting.
- **Job evaluation** is the formal and systematic comparison of a firm's positions. It attempts to compare the effort, responsibility, and skills required to perform each job; compensation for each position is based on job evaluation.
- An organization's **compensation policies** classify it as a pay leader, market rate, or pay follower.
- Employees are either **exempt** or **nonexempt**. The latter is governed by legislation regulating minimum wage, overtime, and other rights and worker protections.
- **Mandatory benefits** include the following: (1) Social Security, (2) unemployment compensation, and (3) workers' compensation. Common discretionary benefits include (1) paid vacations, (2) sick pay, (3) medical benefits, (4) life insurance, (5) retirement plans, (6) stock option plans, (7) childcare, and (8) scholarships for dependents. There are also voluntary benefits, such as vision and dental insurance.
- **The Occupational Safety and Health Administration** (OSHA) is charged with creating safe work environments in U.S. worksites. Areas that companies should focus on to create safe and healthy working conditions are as follows: (1) unsafe worker behavior, (2) unsafe working conditions, (3) Job Hazard Analysis to assess worksites, (4) ergonomics, and (5) accident investigation.
- **Quality of work life** is the extent to which employees can enhance their personal lives through their work environment and experiences.
- **Employment law** is divided into four categories: (1) equal employment, (2) compensation and benefits, (3) health, safety, and employee rights, and (4) unions.
- **Labor unions** strive to improve wages, hours, working conditions, and benefits for their members. A union contract generally covers such issues as wages and overtime and such special situations as hazard pay, layoff or severance pay, holidays, vacations, and family care provisions.
- HRM assists **multinational organizations** to recruit, select, assist, and train employees for working abroad. Among the factors that HRM on the global level must deal with are **culture, different legal systems, political risks**, and **different economic systems**.
- Current HRM issues and trends to monitor include **human resource information systems, changing patterns of work relationships, the global HR environment, social media**, and **corporate social responsibility and sustainability**.

Chapter 4

Human Resource Management Post-Test

POST-TEST ANSWER SHEET

1. Ⓐ Ⓑ Ⓒ Ⓓ	17. Ⓐ Ⓑ Ⓒ Ⓓ	33. Ⓐ Ⓑ Ⓒ Ⓓ
2. Ⓐ Ⓑ Ⓒ Ⓓ	18. Ⓐ Ⓑ Ⓒ Ⓓ	34. Ⓐ Ⓑ Ⓒ Ⓓ
3. Ⓐ Ⓑ Ⓒ Ⓓ	19. Ⓐ Ⓑ Ⓒ Ⓓ	35. Ⓐ Ⓑ Ⓒ Ⓓ
4. Ⓐ Ⓑ Ⓒ Ⓓ	20. Ⓐ Ⓑ Ⓒ Ⓓ	36. Ⓐ Ⓑ Ⓒ Ⓓ
5. Ⓐ Ⓑ Ⓒ Ⓓ	21. Ⓐ Ⓑ Ⓒ Ⓓ	37. Ⓐ Ⓑ Ⓒ Ⓓ
6. Ⓐ Ⓑ Ⓒ Ⓓ	22. Ⓐ Ⓑ Ⓒ Ⓓ	38. Ⓐ Ⓑ Ⓒ Ⓓ
7. Ⓐ Ⓑ Ⓒ Ⓓ	23. Ⓐ Ⓑ Ⓒ Ⓓ	39. Ⓐ Ⓑ Ⓒ Ⓓ
8. Ⓐ Ⓑ Ⓒ Ⓓ	24. Ⓐ Ⓑ Ⓒ Ⓓ	40. Ⓐ Ⓑ Ⓒ Ⓓ
9. Ⓐ Ⓑ Ⓒ Ⓓ	25. Ⓐ Ⓑ Ⓒ Ⓓ	41. Ⓐ Ⓑ Ⓒ Ⓓ
10. Ⓐ Ⓑ Ⓒ Ⓓ	26. Ⓐ Ⓑ Ⓒ Ⓓ	42. Ⓐ Ⓑ Ⓒ Ⓓ
11. Ⓐ Ⓑ Ⓒ Ⓓ	27. Ⓐ Ⓑ Ⓒ Ⓓ	43. Ⓐ Ⓑ Ⓒ Ⓓ
12. Ⓐ Ⓑ Ⓒ Ⓓ	28. Ⓐ Ⓑ Ⓒ Ⓓ	44. Ⓐ Ⓑ Ⓒ Ⓓ
13. Ⓐ Ⓑ Ⓒ Ⓓ	29. Ⓐ Ⓑ Ⓒ Ⓓ	45. Ⓐ Ⓑ Ⓒ Ⓓ
14. Ⓐ Ⓑ Ⓒ Ⓓ	30. Ⓐ Ⓑ Ⓒ Ⓓ	46. Ⓐ Ⓑ Ⓒ Ⓓ
15. Ⓐ Ⓑ Ⓒ Ⓓ	31. Ⓐ Ⓑ Ⓒ Ⓓ	47. Ⓐ Ⓑ Ⓒ Ⓓ
16. Ⓐ Ⓑ Ⓒ Ⓓ	32. Ⓐ Ⓑ Ⓒ Ⓓ	48. Ⓐ Ⓑ Ⓒ Ⓓ

49. Ⓐ Ⓑ Ⓒ Ⓓ   **53.** Ⓐ Ⓑ Ⓒ Ⓓ   **57.** Ⓐ Ⓑ Ⓒ Ⓓ

50. Ⓐ Ⓑ Ⓒ Ⓓ   **54.** Ⓐ Ⓑ Ⓒ Ⓓ   **58.** Ⓐ Ⓑ Ⓒ Ⓓ

51. Ⓐ Ⓑ Ⓒ Ⓓ   **55.** Ⓐ Ⓑ Ⓒ Ⓓ   **59.** Ⓐ Ⓑ Ⓒ Ⓓ

52. Ⓐ Ⓑ Ⓒ Ⓓ   **56.** Ⓐ Ⓑ Ⓒ Ⓓ   **60.** Ⓐ Ⓑ Ⓒ Ⓓ

HUMAN RESOURCE MANAGEMENT POST-TEST

72 minutes—60 questions

Directions: Carefully read each of the following 60 questions. Choose the best answer to each question and fill in the corresponding circle on the answer sheet. The Answer Key and Explanations can be found following this post-test.

---

1. Which of the following is part of the staffing function of HRM?

   A. Reporting workplace accidents
   B. Developing workplace security policies
   C. Motivating employees with career goals
   D. Negotiating compensation with job candidates

2. What must happen before workers have a performance evaluation?

   A. They must be told what their deficiencies are.
   B. They must be told what the performance criteria are.
   C. They must do a self-analysis and share it with the supervisor.
   D. They must be informed of any raise they will receive.

3. Which of the following describes m-learning?

   A. Using a personal computer to access online training portals
   B. Using a smartphone or tablet to access online training portals
   C. Using a company computer to access corporate training modules
   D. Using in-person orientation sessions to access training modules

4. Accidents due to unsafe worker behavior often occur

   A. after an OSHA inspection.
   B. right after a job hazard analysis.
   C. during a worker's first few months of employment.
   D. in a series of accidents.

5. Human resources are a company's

A. customers.
B. employees.
C. supervisors.
D. management.

6. A good performance review will depend mainly on whether the worker has

A. met all the objectives expected of him or her.
B. ever been promoted before.
C. been with the firm for twenty or more years.
D. a friendly relationship with his or her supervisor.

7. What is the function of a job analysis?

A. To determine what skills are needed for certain jobs
B. To make employees aware of why they are being terminated
C. To develop pay ranges
D. To create and maintain up-to-date files on each employee

8. What is the first step in a job evaluation?

A. Job analysis
B. Job ranking
C. Pay grade
D. Job description

9. Orientation generally includes

A. a test about the company's expectations about new employees' performance.
B. a chance for new employees to explain what they expect from their employment in the company.
C. six months for new employees to prove their value to the firm.
D. information about the firm's history.

10. What is Frederick Taylor known for?

A. As an industrial psychologist
B. As the founder of scientific management
C. As head of the first craft union
D. As the originator of personnel departments

11. Alternatives to having a supervisor evaluate an employee include all of the following EXCEPT:

   A. Peer reviews
   B. Written tests
   C. Evaluation by subordinates
   D. Appraisal by team members

12. Which of the following would require that a job design be altered?

   A. Procedures and requirements for the job change
   B. New employees replacing more experienced ones
   C. Hiring exceeding demand for products or services
   D. Weaknesses in the workforce revealing themselves

13. How can managers avoid accusations of bias in the evaluation process?

   A. By submitting their critiques in writing to their subordinates
   B. By ignoring minor deficiencies and concentrating on major problems
   C. By acting on problems in all workers' performance as they arise
   D. By having HR sit in all performance appraisals

14. Which of the following describes employment at will?

   A. An employee may not terminate employment unless the company agrees.
   B. An employee may or may not choose to sign a contract of employment.
   C. An employer may terminate an employee for any reason or for no reason.
   D. An employer may revoke an employee's contract.

15. Workplace diversity refers to which of the following?

   A. Employing workers from a range of ages and ethnicities
   B. Seeking highly skilled and knowledgeable employees
   C. Operating both domestically and internationally
   D. Providing multicultural training to employees

16. Which of the following describes the planning function of HRM?

A. Researching wage trends
B. Interviewing job candidates
C. Providing e-learning opportunities
D. Recruiting through social media

17. Which of the following statements is NOT true?

A. A pay grade is made up of all jobs that fall within a certain range.
B. The purpose of a pay curve is to help managers develop a progression between pay grades.
C. Most companies pay one rate for all jobs in a pay grade.
D. A wage curve shows the relative value of all jobs.

18. A reduction in workforce may occur because of

A. a merger with or buyout by another company.
B. attrition.
C. errors in predicting job needs.
D. inadequate training programs to match employees with required skills sets.

19. Generally, unions organize an industry because of dissatisfaction with

A. the job market.
B. the economy.
C. management policies.
D. globalization

20. Which of the following laws is applicable when an employer is planning a mass layoff?

A. NLRA
B. ADA
C. FLSA
D. WARN

21. The Americans with Disabilities Act applies to discrimination against

    A. workers employed by certain federal contractors.
    B. certain age ranges, the ranges changing over time.
    C. retired workers whose funds have been mismanaged.
    D. workers reporting hazards to OSHA.

22. Which of the following objectives would be most helpful in evaluating an employee's performance?

    A. Work efficiently.
    B. Produce the project on time and on budget.
    C. Create a new ad campaign by September 15, 2021.
    D. Develop ten informational fact sheets on Bike X by June 15, 2021.

23. The HR department is able to create a job description by means of

    A. questionnaires.
    B. observation.
    C. interviews of employees in the job.
    D. a combination of questionnaires, observation, and interviews of employees in the job.

24. What is the primary purpose of a job hazard analysis?

    A. To teach workers about ergonomics
    B. To identify work activities that are dangerous
    C. To encourage workers to apply for disability insurance
    D. To monitor workers in their first few months on the job

25. In establishing pay rates, the compensation manager must take into account all of the following factors EXCEPT:

    A. The company's policies on salaries
    B. The company's ability to pay
    C. Movement in the stock market in the short term
    D. What the company president will receive at retirement

26. Which of the following describes a defined benefit plan?

A. The amount that the retiree receives is fixed at a certain amount for life.

B. The amount that the retiree receives depends on how much the company invests for the employee and how well the investment does.

C. A defined benefit plan is another name for a 401(k) plan.

D. It is a trust that holds company stock and divides the stock among employees based on their earnings.

27. Which of the following statements is NOT true about phased retirement?

A. Workers have to retire by age 70.

B. Workers can adjust gradually to a new lifestyle while still working.

C. Workers can reduce their hours but keep their benefits while they continue working.

D. Employers have a ready-made resource for mentoring younger workers by using phased retirement of experienced workers.

28. OSHA provides industry-specific health and safety standards for which type of business?

A. Publishing

B. Construction

C. Auto sales

D. Agriculture

29. The right of labor to organize and engage in collective bargaining is covered by which of the following laws?

A. Employee Retirement Income Security Act

B. National Labor Relations Act

C. Age Discrimination in Employment Act

D. Taft-Hartley Act

30. Human Resource Information Systems allow for the

A. control of internet communications.

B. setting up of virtual offices.

C. collection and storage of vast amounts of data.

D. monitoring of flexplace and flextime work arrangements.

31. Which of the following describes trend analysis for forecasting staffing needs?

   A. HRM develops a forecast based on the ratio between factors.
   B. HRM considers current factors to determine future staffing needs.
   C. HRM creates a visual representation of variables, such as the number of departments in an organization and the number of employees in each department.
   D. HRM looks at staffing needs in an organization's departments over a period of time.

32. In collective bargaining, it is important that

   A. all union member employees be present at the negotiations.
   B. grievances be settled first.
   C. both sides be willing to make concessions.
   D. both sides agree on whether or not the business will be a closed shop.

33. According to the ADEA, an employer is prohibited from discriminating against which of the following?

   A. Employees who have a disability
   B. Employees who take maternity leave
   C. Employees who are aged 40 or older
   D. Employees who belong to a union

34. Which of the following describes an autonomous work group?

   A. Team of workers deciding for themselves how to handle work assignments
   B. Third-party contracted work team
   C. An outsourcing group
   D. A professional employer organization

35. Which law has been most effective in limiting discrimination in the workplace?

   A. Fair Labor Standards Act
   B. Civil Service Reform Act
   C. National Labor Relations Act
   D. Civil Rights Act Title VII

36. Outplacement is a company's way of trying to

    A. reduce the size of its staff through voluntary turnover.
    B. help terminated workers strengthen their job-search skills.
    C. learn how workers feel about how the firm treated them.
    D. gauge how much turnover there has been.

37. Which of the following is a provision of the Taft-Hartley Act?

    A. Employees could refuse to join a union.
    B. Unions no longer had to give employers notice of an impending strike.
    C. The US president was no longer allowed to halt a strike on the basis of a national emergency.
    D. Employers may not publicize negative opinions about unions among their workers.

38. Which of the following could result in a wrongful termination suit?

    A. The company did not adhere to guarantees made to the employee when hiring.
    B. The company found unexplained gaps in an applicant's employment.
    C. The company does not train workers in conflict management.
    D. The company does not guarantee worker safety.

39. Surveys presented at the end of a training experience measure

    A. the need for additional training.
    B. immediate feedback on the program.
    C. changes in the participants' behaviors.
    D. changes in the results that the organization is experiencing because of the training.

40. What was the primary goal of Frederick Taylor's theory of management?

    A. Measuring product quality
    B. Improving labor productivity
    C. Reducing the workforce
    D. Evaluating employee performance

41. What does a right-to-work law do?

    A. Requires employers to hire only union members
    B. Removes the right to strike from unions
    C. Removes the requirement that workers in a union shop pay
        union dues whether they belong to the union or not
    D. Requires that the union steward negotiate wages for all workers

42. The four-fifths rule is used to determine which of the following?

    A. Wage rates
    B. Workplace diversity
    C. Adverse impact
    D. Performance rankings

43. Worker development is concerned mainly with

    A. fine-tuning employees' current skills sets.
    B. employee job satisfaction.
    C. employees' future career paths.
    D. improving employee weaknesses.

44. A company that is paying the market rate in salaries is

    A. paying no more than average.
    B. paying less than all its competitors.
    C. paying the highest compensation in the field.
    D. attracting the most highly qualified workers.

45. What is the purpose of exit interviews of workers who leave an organization voluntarily?

    A. To gain insight on why they are leaving
    B. To have them fill out termination paperwork
    C. To try to persuade them to stay by offering incentives
    D. To ask them to recommend replacements

46. Which of the following is NOT a category analyzed for hazards under OSHA regulations?

    A. Walking surfaces
    B. Emergency exits
    C. Coin-operated machines
    D. Electrical systems

47. Which of the following is a true statement about performance appraisals (PAs)?

   A. The basis for evaluation at a PA is the set of goals the employee and supervisor set at the last PA.
   B. The supervisor prepares all paperwork for a PA.
   C. Supervisors are more likely to schedule PAs with employees who have problems in order to get them over with.
   D. Rating all employees in a department as average favors all the employees.

48. Which performance appraisal method focuses on the behaviors necessary for a specific position or job task at a firm?

   A. Assessment center method
   B. MBO
   C. Forced distribution method
   D. BARS

49. An organization would likely use a staffing firm for which of the following purposes?

   A. To fill high-level positions
   B. To hire temporary workers
   C. To manage payroll issues
   D. To recruit on college campuses

50. What development made the passage of ERISA necessary?

   A. Compensation and benefits programs became too expensive for most organizations.
   B. Health, safety, and employee rights were being abused by companies.
   C. Some retirement funds were mismanaged, and workers lost their retirement benefits.
   D. Union contracts did not cover members' retirement needs.

51. The principle of transfer of learning means that workers

   A. are motivated to continually learn new skills.
   B. learn by asking questions of mentors.
   C. can avoid being locked into one career path.
   D. must inform management of their online studies.

52. An agreement between a company and a labor union typically covers

    A. check card procedures.
    B. overtime pay.
    C. arbitration procedures.
    D. closed shop provisions.

53. Which of the following best describes disparate impact discrimination?

    A. A supervisor harasses a female employee because of her gender.
    B. African-American job applicants are tested for specific job skills at a higher rate than applicants of other racial groups.
    C. A supervisor harasses a Catholic employee because of his religion.
    D. Muslim job applicants are hired at a lower rate compared to other ethnic groups because of unintentional flaws in the selection process.

54. Which situation or condition would most likely attract an OSHA inspector's attention?

    A. No employees over the age of 40
    B. Lack of any retirement program
    C. Foreign-born workers who do not speak English
    D. The lack of well-marked emergency exits

55. The categories of exempt and nonexempt workers differ in that

    A. nonexempt employees are covered by laws regulating minimum wage.
    B. neither category is defined by legislation.
    C. exempt employees receive an hourly wage and nonexempt employees receive salaries.
    D. nonexempt employees include outside salespeople, which is not a category of exempt workers.

56. Which performance appraisal method relies on feedback from an employee's managers, co-workers, and direct reports?

    A. 360-degree appraisal
    B. Critical incident method
    C. Grading method
    D. Paired comparison approach

57. Employee stock ownership plans are a form of

    A. monetary compensation.
    B. gift certificates.
    C. commissions.
    D. nonmonetary compensation.

58. Which statement about the FMLA is true?

    A. The FMLA applies to personal and family illnesses.
    B. The FMLA is limited to government employees.
    C. The FMLA provides six weeks of paid maternity leave.
    D. The FMLA applies to employers with at least 20 employees

59. E-learning for employees is popular because

    A. it is highly flexible.
    B. it is easy.
    C. it is not costly to prepare or purchase training materials.
    D. of its lack of assessments and tests.

60. Which of the following is true about workers' compensation?

    A. It pays benefits to workers who lose their jobs in a recession.
    B. It is similar to Social Security payments.
    C. It is a form of disability insurance.
    D. It reimburses a worker for expenses incurred in a job-related accident.

ANSWER KEY AND EXPLANATIONS

1. D	13. C	25. C	37. A	49. B
2. B	14. C	26. A	38. A	50. C
3. B	15. A	27. A	39. B	51. C
4. C	16. A	28. B	40. B	52. B
5. B	17. C	29. B	41. C	53. D
6. A	18. A	30. C	42. C	54. D
7. A	19. C	31. D	43. C	55. A
8. A	20. D	32. C	44. A	56. A
9. D	21. A	33. C	45. A	57. D
10. B	22. D	34. A	46. C	58. A
11. B	23. D	35. D	47. A	59. A
12. A	24. B	36. B	48. D	60. D

1. **The correct answer is D.** The staffing function relates to the hiring process and includes recruiting employees and negotiating compensation. Choices A and B relate to the function of protecting workers, not hiring them. While motivating employees is an important HRM task, doing so is not part of the staffing function, which makes choice C incorrect.

2. **The correct answer is B.** Before a performance evaluation occurs, workers must be told what the performance criteria are. Choice A is incorrect because discussion of deficiencies happens during a performance appraisal, not before. Choice C is incorrect because self-analyses are not shared with supervisors. Choice D is incorrect because that happens during or after the evaluation, but not before.

3. **The correct answer is B.** M-learning is short for mobile learning, which occurs on mobile devices such as smartphones, tablets, or laptops. A personal computer (choice A) and a company computer (choice C) are not terms associated with mobile devices. Choice D is incorrect because m-learning occurs remotely rather than in-person.

4. The correct answer is C. Accidents due to unsafe work behavior often occur during a worker's first few months of employment. Choices A and B are incorrect because there is no evidence to support a causal relationship between OSHA inspections and accidents, nor between a job hazard analysis and accidents. Choice D is incorrect because there is no evidence to support the idea that accidents happen in a series.

5. The correct answer is B. Human resources are a company's employees. Choice A is incorrect because customers are not part of the organization. Choices C and D are incorrect because while supervisors and management are part of an organization's human resources, they are only parts.

6. The correct answer is A. A good performance review will mainly depend upon whether the worker has met all the expected objectives. A good performance review does not typically focus on past promotions (choice B), or length of time with a company (choice C). A friendly relationship with a supervisor (choice D) could result in a subjective performance appraisal by the supervisor.

7. The correct answer is A. A job analysis determines what skills are needed for certain jobs. Choice B is incorrect because a performance evaluation, not a job analysis, would be useful in explaining why an employee is being terminated. Choice C is incorrect because a salary survey and a job evaluation are used to help determine pay ranges, not a job analysis. Choice D is incorrect because the analysis is independent of any single employee's records.

8. The correct answer is A. The job evaluation process begins with the creation of a job analysis for each position. This information is then used to create a job description (choice D). HR will use job ranking (choice B) to place jobs in an order from highest to lowest, which is helpful in assigning a pay grade (choice C).

9. **The correct answer is D.** The purpose of orientation is to provide new employees with information about their employer. Orientations are not presented in the form of a test (choice A), nor are they a forum for discussing what new employees expect from their employment (choice B). Choice C is incorrect because proving an employee's value to a company is a matter of working for the company, not learning about it.

10. **The correct answer is B.** Frederick Taylor is known as the founder of scientific management. He was not an industrial psychologist (choice A) and he was not involved in the union movement (choice C). The first craft unions were founded in Great Britain and the United States in the mid-1800s. The largest in the United States was the American Federation of Labor, which organized a federation of craft unions in 1886. Choice D is incorrect because Taylor was not involved in the development of personnel departments, which came much later than Taylor, who died in 1915.

11. **The correct answer is B.** You're looking for the wrong answer in *except* and *not* questions, and the answer that doesn't fit in this series is choice B. Written tests are not used as an alternative to having a supervisor evaluate an employee. Peer reviews (choice A), subordinates' evaluating an employee who reports to a higher-level supervisor (choice C), and team member appraisals (choice D) are alternative methods of employee evaluation.

12. **The correct answer is A.** Procedures and requirements for a job change would trigger that a job design needs to be altered. New employees replacing more experienced ones (choice B) would not affect job design. Having too many employees for the amount of work required to meet demand (choice C) would affect staffing, but not job design. Weaknesses in the workforce (choice D) should not be remedied by changing the job design.

13. **The correct answer is C.** Managers can avoid accusations of bias in the evaluation process by acting on problems with workers as issues arise. Submitting critiques in writing to subordinates (choice A) is not a effective solution and could possibly contribute to an accusation of bias. Ignoring minor deficiencies and concentrating on major problems (choice B) would not be helpful to the employee, the supervisor, or the organization. Having HR sit in all performance reviews (choice D) is not a practical solution.

14. **The correct answer is C.** Employment at will means that there is no written contract between employee and employer that specifies a set period of employment. Either party may terminate employment at any time; the employer may or may not give a reason for termination. Choice A is incorrect because employment at will doesn't require the agreement of the employer. Choices B and D are incorrect because there is no contract involved in employment at will.

15. **The correct answer is A.** A diverse organization has employees of different ages, genders, ethnicities, religious backgrounds, and physical abilities. Although most organizations seek highly skilled employees, doing so doesn't mean a company is diverse, which makes choice B incorrect. The location of a company's business does not relate to its diversity, so choice C is incorrect. Multicultural training may or may not be offered by a diverse organization, so choice D is incorrect.

16. **The correct answer is A.** The planning function of HRM involves tasks such as researching wage trends and monitoring the labor market. Interviewing job candidates (choice B) and recruiting through social media (choice D) relate to the staffing function of HRM. The development function of HRM involves providing training opportunities (choice C).

17. **The correct answer is C.** This question is asking for the statement among the answer choices that is false. The statements in choices A, B, and D are all true, which leaves choice C as the false statement.

18. **The correct answer is A.** A reduction in workforce may be triggered by a merger with another company or in a buyout situation. Attrition (choice B) is not hiring employees to replace those who leave voluntarily or are terminated for cause. It is a method used as an alternative to a RIF. It is likely that an error in predicting job needs (choice C) would be corrected by other means, such as choice B, before a RIF would be necessary. Choice D is incorrect because training programs would be revised before employees would be let go.

19. **The correct answer is C.** Unions typically are organized in an industry in response to overall dissatisfaction and disillusion with management policies. The job market (choice A), the economy (choice B), or globalization (choice D) could factor in to the decision to organize, but would not have as direct of an influence as dissatisfaction with management policies.

20. **The correct answer is D.** The Worker Adjustment and Retraining Notification Act (WARN) requires employers to give employees 60 days' notice before a plant closing or mass layoff. The National Labor Relations Act (NLRA) supports the right to organize, so choice A is incorrect. The Americans with Disabilities Act (ADA) prohibits discrimination against applicants with disabilities, and the Fair Labor Standards Act (FLSA) relates to wages and working conditions, which means choices B and C are incorrect.

21. **The correct answer is A.** The ADA applies to discrimination against workers employed by certain federal contractors. Choice B is incorrect because age discrimination is prohibited under the Age Discrimination in Employment Act (ADEA). Choice C is incorrect because pensions are guaranteed under the Employment Retirement Income Security Act (ERISA). Choice D is incorrect because the Occupational Safety and Health Administration (OSHA) deals with issues of worker safety and health.

22. **The correct answer is D.** Employee objectives need to be clearly stated and quantifiable. Only choice D meets both criteria. Choice A can be eliminated because it is vague, as is choice B. Choice C is better, but doesn't indicate what the ad campaign is for.

23. **The correct answer is D.** Choices A, B, and C alone are not the best answers. The best answer combines all three: questionnaires, observation, and interviews.

24. **The correct answer is B.** The primary purpose of a job hazard analysis is to identify dangerous work activities. Choice A is incorrect because ergonomics refers to only one issue considered in identifying workplace hazards. Choice C is incorrect because disability coverage is provided through workers' comp, which almost all companies must carry by law; some companies also buy additional disability insurance for employees. Although many accidents may occur in a worker's first few months, choice D is not the best answer because the primary purpose of job hazard analysis is to protect all workers.

25. **The correct answer is C.** Movement in the stock market doesn't usually affect company policy on salaries in the short term. Choice A is incorrect because a company's policies on salaries are something the compensation manager must take into account. Choice B is incorrect because the company's ability to pay is something that does affect salaries. Choice D is incorrect because even if the company president's retirement benefits are expensive, they are not covered under salary policies.

26. **The correct answer is A.** A defined benefit plan means that the amount the retiree receives is fixed at a certain amount for life. This type of plan was the typical pension plan for companies that offered pensions to their employees. Today, companies are moving to choice B, which describes a defined contribution plan. Choice C is incorrect because a 401(k) plan is a type of defined benefit plan, not the definition of. Choice D describes an employee stock option plan (ESOP).

27. **The correct answer is A.** There is no set age for retirement; however, age 70 is the age at which people must begin taking their Social Security benefits. Note that although working fewer hours means a reduction in pay, employees keep their benefits. Choices B, C, and D are all true statements.

28. The correct answer is B. The dangerous nature of the construction industry has resulted in specific health and safety guidelines from OSHA. Businesses in the publishing, sales, and farming industries must comply with general OSHA guidelines but lack specific standards, so choices A, C, and D are incorrect.

29. The correct answer is B. The National Labor Relations Act covers the right of labor to organize and engage in collective bargaining. ERISA (choice A) deals with retirement programs. ADEA (choice C) deals with discrimination against workers within certain age ranges. The Taft-Hartley Act (choice D) deals mainly with unfair union labor practices and also enumerates the rights of employees and employers.

30. The correct answer is C. Human Resource Information Systems allow for the collection and storage of vast amounts of data. HRIS does not control internet communications (choice A) and setting up virtual offices (choice B) isn't its purpose. HRIS does not monitor flexplace and flextime work arrangements (choice D), though it may collect data about them.

31. The correct answer is D. Trend analysis forecasting is concerned with identifying patterns over a period of time, not just current factors (choice B), that might affect future staffing needs. Forecasting by calculating a ratio between a specific business variable and the number of employees needed (choice A) describes ratio analysis. Forecasting by creating a visual representation of variables (choice C) describes scatter plot analysis.

32. The correct answer is C. In order to come to an agreement, both sides must be willing to make concessions and act in good faith. The shop steward represents the workers during negotiations, so there is no need for all employees to attend (choice A). Settling of grievances (choice B) is a procedure that is clarified in the collective bargaining agreements, not a prerequisite of the process itself. Closed shops (choice D) are illegal, so the subject would be no part of the negotiations.

33. **The correct answer is C.** The Age Discrimination in Employment Act (ADEA) prohibits discrimination based on age. Choice A is incorrect because the Americans with Disabilities Act (ADA) prohibits discrimination against applicants with disabilities. Choice B is covered by the Family and Medical Leave Act (FMLA). Choice D is incorrect because labor laws such as the NLRA protect union members.

34. **The correct answer is A.** An autonomous work group is a team of workers deciding for themselves how to handle work assignments. Choices B and C describe outsourcing. Choice D is incorrect because a PEO hires employees laid off by a company, pays them and their benefits, and leases their services to companies.

35. **The correct answer is D.** The Civil Rights Act Title VII has been the most effective in limiting discrimination in the workplace. The FLSA (choice A) deals mainly with minimum wage, maximum hours, overtime pay, equal pay, record keeping, and child labor provisions, as well as distinguishing between exempt and nonexempt employees. The CSRA (choice B) is concerned with labor management relations in the federal service. The NLRA (choice C) supports the right of labor to organize and engage in collective bargaining.

36. **The correct answer is B.** Outplacement is a company's way of trying to help terminated workers strengthen their job-search skills. Outplacement is not related to voluntary turnover (choice A). Learning how terminated employees feel about the company (choice C) is the purpose of the exit interview. Choice D is incorrect because turnover generally relates to voluntary termination, whereas outsourcing is for workers terminated involuntarily. Also, outplacement has nothing to do with monitoring.

37. **The correct answer is A.** By giving workers the right to not join a union, the Taft-Hartley Act banned the closed shop. Choice B is incorrect because unions are required under the law to notify a company 60 days in advance of an impending strike. Choice C is incorrect because it is the opposite of what the law says; the US president may intervene and apply for an injunction to halt the strike. Choice D is incorrect because the Taft-Hartley Act allows employers to give their side of what unionization may do to the company and to their jobs in the future.

38. **The correct answer is A.** A wrongful termination suit is brought by a former employee. Choice B is incorrect because unexplained gaps should be apparent on a person's resume and be dealt with during an interview. Also, it is illogical to consider that a former employee would begin a lawsuit because of an omission on his or her part. Choice C is incorrect because conflict management training is not a requirement. Choice D is incorrect because not guaranteeing worker safety is illegal.

39. **The correct answer is B.** Surveys presented at the end of a training experience are designed to provide immediate feedback on the program. Choice A is incorrect because the need for additional training will be measured on how well participants learned the information and put it into practice. Choice C is incorrect because any possible changes in behavior related to the training have not yet taken place. Choice D is incorrect because the employees have not yet had an opportunity to put into practice—or not—what they've learned during the training.

40. **The correct answer is B.** In his scientific management theory, Taylor proposed that labor productivity would improve if work processes were simplified. Taylor did not try to quantify product quality, so choice A is incorrect. Improving efficiency rather than reducing the workforce was the focus of Taylor's theory, so choice C is incorrect. Choice D is incorrect because Taylor focused on work processes rather than individual employees.

41. **The correct answer is C.** A right-to-work law removes the requirement that workers in a union shop pay union dues whether they belong to the union or not. Choice A is incorrect because employers can hire both union and nonunion workers regardless of whether a state has a right-to-work law. Choice B is incorrect because right-to-work laws are state laws, and federal law guarantees the right to strike; federal law takes precedence over state law. Choice D is incorrect because the union has a panel of union members that negotiate contract terms, including wages.

42. **The correct answer is C.** The four-fifths rule is the primary method of determining adverse impact, which refers to hiring practices that seem neutral but actually discriminate against a protected group. Wage rates (choice A) and workplace diversity (choice B) are HRM planning issues. Performance rankings (choice D) are a part of HRM staffing issues.

43. **The correct answer is C.** Worker development is primarily concerned with employees' future career paths. Choice A is incorrect because development is mainly concerned with future skills, not present skills; improving skills is the work of training programs. Choice B is incorrect because worker development is concerned with future positions, not current job satisfaction. Choice D is incorrect because although an employee's weaknesses are of concern, strengthening skills and knowledge would be only one part of the plan for his or her future and would involve training.

44. **The correct answer is A.** A company that is paying the market rate in salaries is paying no more than average. Choice B describes a pay follower. Choice C describes a pay leader. Choice D is incorrect because it is unlikely that a company paying average compensation would attract the most highly qualified workers.

45. **The correct answer is A.** The purpose of an exit interview for a worker who is voluntarily leaving is to gain insight on why the employee is leaving. While an employee may need to fill out paperwork (choice B), this is not the intended purpose of an exit interview. Choice C is incorrect because it is not the place of HRM to offer incentives; that would be done by the supervisor, if interested, at the time the employee resigns. While choice D may occur, it is not the purpose of an exit interview.

46. **The correct answer is C.** While it is possible that an employee might get his or her hand caught in a vending machine, vending machines are not a category of hazards under OSHA regulations.

47. **The correct answer is A.** The basis for evaluation at a PA is the set of goals the employee and supervisor set at the last PA. Choice B is incorrect because the employee completes his or her own evaluation form, which will be used with the supervisor's during the PA interview. Choice C is incorrect because human nature being what it is, supervisors who have to deliver unpleasant information tend to put off those PAs. Choice D is known as the central tendency error and is incorrect because it favors the underachiever, but not the overachiever.

48. **The correct answer is D.** The Behaviorally Anchored Rating Scales (BARS) method compares employee performance against specific job-related behaviors. Choice A is incorrect because assessment centers use multiple evaluation methods and do not focus only on job task behaviors. The management by objectives method (choice B) focuses on goal setting rather than behaviors. Forced distribution (choice C) is a method of ranking employees after they have been evaluated.

49. **The correct answer is B.** Staffing firms are often used to fill short-term or temporary positions at a company. Executive search firms specialize in filling executive positions, so choice A is incorrect. Staffing firms fill open positions and do not handle payroll problems (choice C). A firm's HR personnel typically recruits on college campuses, so choice D is incorrect.

50. **The correct answer is C.** ERISA is the Employment Retirement Income Security Act, which protects retirement funds. The fact that some retirement funds were mismanaged and workers lost their retirement benefits spurred the development and passage of ERISA. Choice A is incorrect because the passage of ERISA was separate from the cost of compensation and benefits packages. Choice B is incorrect because ERISA deals only with retirement benefits. Choice D is incorrect because union contracts usually do cover retirement benefits.

51. **The correct answer is C.** The principle of transfer of learning means that workers can avoid being locked into one career path. Choice A is incorrect because transfer of skills involves taking what one has learned in one job to a new job. Choice B is incorrect because transfer of skills does not refer to passing on information, but to applying it to a new position. Choice D is incorrect because transfer of learning has nothing to do with a requirement for employees to inform management when they take courses.

52. **The correct answer is B.** An agreement between a company and a labor union typically covers overtime pay. Choice A is incorrect because the check card, or authorization card, is part of the process of organizing a workplace by a union. It is used in place of an election to determine if the workers wish to unionize. Choice C is incorrect because any arbitration procedure is set at the time of contract negotiation. Choice D is incorrect because a closed shop is illegal and could not be part of a bargaining agreement.

53. **The correct answer is D.** Disparate treatment discrimination involves intentionally discriminating against employees or job applicants because of their race, religion, or gender. Disparate impact discrimination is unintentional. Choices A, B, and C reflect situations of disparate treatment. Choice D reflects disparate impact discrimination.

54. **The correct answer is D.** The lack of well-marked emergency exits would attract the attention of an OSHA inspector. Choice A is incorrect because OSHA is concerned with worker safety, not age discrimination, which is the responsibility of the ADEA. Choice B is incorrect because OSHA is concerned with hazardous working conditions, not retirement funds. Choice C is incorrect because OSHA is concerned with workplace injuries and illnesses, not foreign-born workers who may or may not be illegal, unless they are affected by those injuries or illnesses.

55. **The correct answer is A.** Nonexempt employees are covered by laws regulating minimum wage. Choice B is incorrect because the categories are defined by legislation. This answer choice is also wrong because the question asks about the difference between the two categories and this answer choice gives a similarity. Choice C is incorrect because the opposite is true; nonexempt employees receive an hourly wage and exempt employees receive salaries. Choice D is incorrect because nonexempt employees don't include outside salespeople; they belong in the category of exempt workers.

56. **The correct answer is A.** The 360-degree approach utilizes performance feedback from co-workers, customers, direct reports, and managers. In the critical incident method (choice B), one rater evaluates an employee's key job behaviors. The grading method (choice C) involves a manager assigning grades to an employee for specific performance categories. The paired comparison method (choice D) compares the performance of two employees, but only one rater is involved.

57. **The correct answer is D.** ESOPs are a form of nonmonetary compensation. Choice A is incorrect because stock options are not considered monetary compensation. Choice B is incorrect because stock options are not in the form of gift certificates. Choice C is incorrect because commissions are not the same as stock options.

58. **The correct answer is A.** The Family and Medical Leave Act (FMLA) provides leave for childbirth, adoption, and illness. FMLA applies to public and private employers with at least 50 employees, so choices B and D are incorrect. The FMLA allows 12 weeks of unpaid leave, so choice C is incorrect.

59. **The correct answer is A.** E-learning is popular with employees due to its flexibility. Choice B is incorrect because e-learning can be on the level of college courses. Choice C is incorrect because preparing or purchasing training materials can be expensive, though over time, e-learning can be cost-effective, if enough employees use the programs. Choice D is incorrect because e-learning may have assessments and tests, depending on the type of training involved.

60. **The correct answer is D.** Workers' compensation is an insurance program that companies with a certain number of minimum employees must carry to pay medical, death, and income benefits to workers who are injured on the job or contract work-related illnesses. But it is not the same as disability insurance (choice C). Workers' compensation isn't related to job loss from a recession (choice A), nor is it related to Social Security payments (choice B).

CPSIA information can be obtained
at www.ICGtesting.com
Printed in the USA
JSHW041313190722
28277JS00007B/152